Poetry Please!

Popular poems from the
BBC Radio 4 programme

Foreword by
Charles Causley

PHOENIX

Poetry Please! first published in Great Britain in 1985
This abridged edition first published in Everyman in 1996
Phoenix edition first published in 2002

10 9 8 7

A CIP catalogue reference for this book is
available from the British Library.

The Orion Publishing Group
Orion House
5 Upper St Martin's Lane
London
WC2H 9EA

ISBN-13 978-0-7538-1651-6
ISBN-10 0-7538-1651-2

Typeset by Deltatype Ltd,
Birkenhead, Merseyside
Printed in Great Britain by
Clays Ltd, St Ives plc

The Orion Publishing Group's policy is to use papers that
are natural, renewable and recyclable products and
made from wood grown in sustainable forests. The logging
and manufacturing processes are expected to conform to
the environmental regulations of the country of origin.

www.orionbooks.co.uk

Contents

Foreword

As a popular radio programme, *Poetry Please!* owes its inception to Brian Patten, a BBC staff producer based in Bristol. Like many an excellent idea it seems, in retrospect, also a perfectly simple one, and the wonder is that it hadn't been put into action before. But this is not to allow for Brian Patten's quite exceptional energy, imaginative sensibility, and 'feel' for an audience.

Initially planned as a series of eight programmes, the first was broadcast on Radio 4 from the BBC Network Production Centre at Bristol in October, 1979. The series was an immediate success. It returned in 1980 and is still on the air.

The format is simplicity itself: a half-hour programme featuring poems requested by listeners, and read by professional performers. The programme is now presented by the writer and broadcaster Roger McGough.

From the beginning, response from listeners was considerable. Thousands of different poems have been asked for, a great number of them many times over. The following selection of poems most frequently requested has been made by Margaret Bradley, a former producer of *Poetry Please!*, and Peter Shellard of Messrs J. M. Dent and Sons.

The Greek origin of the word 'anthology', in the sense that it is a collection of flowers, reminds us that the conventionally-edited selection is, more often than not, the work of one hand. In such cases, the poems chosen may declare themselves well enough, but the choice itself, as with a bunch of flowers, remains something personally distinctive; often fascinatingly self-revelatory.

The poems always aside, to me the most interesting feature of the *Poetry Please!* anthology is the fact that the various choices were made in the first place by a large number of people by no means all connected necessarily with what might be called the poetry business. Of all the literary arts, poetry – aided by the invaluable mnemonics of rhyme, rhythm and musicality – is something most of us carry in the body's luggage from childhood as, among much else, an affirmative of joy and as a spell against the dark. The poems themselves, or such fragments as we remember, may be great, not so great, the lightest of light verse, or mere jingle: but this is unimportant. What must always be remembered is that no poet in his senses ever wrote for the examination syllabus or the academic dissecting-table. A poem is, in essence, a private communication between a poet and single member of his or her audience. What the reader makes of it, just how it is interpreted, the secret nature of its 'meaning', is for the reader alone, and with perfect validity, to resolve in accordance with an individual experience of life and a personal imagination.

Many of the poems following are well-known and well-loved. Not a few are also often extremely difficult to track down if general collections by their authors are no longer in print. Thomas Hardy once remarked of his own verse that he hoped for a few poems in a good anthology. Such modesty does great credit to Hardy, who as a poet rarely, if ever, faltered in excellence. But it is a fact that out of very large bodies of work, many poets have proved at their best in only a handful of poems. It is often through the work of the anthologist, then, as well as from the active and passionate desire of the individual reader to share an enthusiasm with others, that such poems are afforded a well-deserved continuance of light and life in print along with the work of the poets of consistent and supreme genius.

It was Dickens's Tony Weller, in *The Pickwick Papers*, who struck a note of anxiety when his son Sam received a Valentine:

> 'Tain't in poetry, is it?'
> 'No, no,' replied Sam.
> 'Wery glad to hear it,' said Mr Weller. 'Poetry's unnat'ral; no man ever talked poetry 'cept a beadle on boxin' day, or Warren's blackin', or Rowland's oil, or some o' them low fellows; never you let yourself down to talk poetry, my boy . . .'

Poetry Please!, whether in print or on the air, gives the lie to such subversive sentiments. Sadly, Brian Patten did not live to see the publication of the present collection, though he was much involved in the early stages of its preparation. To me, the happiest tribute to the memory of a delightful man is the appearance of *Poetry Please!*: an anthology of what, by its very origins, may be described as truly popular verse.

CHARLES CAUSLEY

Poetry Please!

For Brian Patten,
whose idea *Poetry Please!* was —
a very special BBC producer

Indian Prayer (traditional)

ANON

When I am dead
Cry for me a little
Think of me sometimes
But not too much.
Think of me now and again
As I was in life
At some moments it's pleasant to recall
But not for long.
Leave me in peace
And I shall leave you in peace
And while you live
Let your thoughts be with the living.

from Miss Thompson Goes Shopping

MARTIN ARMSTRONG

In her lone cottage on the downs,
With winds and blizzards and great crowns
Of shining cloud, with wheeling plover
And short grass sweet with the small white clover,
Miss Thompson lived, correct and meek,
A lonely spinster, and every week
On market-day she used to go
Into the little town below,
Tucked in the great downs' hollow bowl,
Like pebbles gathered in a shoal.

So, having washed her plates and cup
And banked the kitchen fire up,
Miss Thompson slipped upstairs and dressed,
Put on her black (her second best),
The bonnet trimmed with rusty plush,
Peeped in the glass with simpering blush,
From camphor-smelling cupboard took
Her thicker jacket off the hook
Because the day might turn to cold.
Then, ready, slipped downstairs and rolled
The hearthrug back; then searched about,
Found her basket, ventured out,
Snecked the door and paused to lock it
And plunged the key in some deep pocket.

Then as she tripped demurely down
The steep descent, the little town

Spread wider till its sprawling street
Enclosed her and her footfalls beat
On hard stone pavement; and she felt
Those throbbing ecstasies that melt
Through heart and mind, as, happy, free,
Her small, prim personality
Merged into the seething strife
Of auction-marts and city life.

The Forsaken Merman

MATTHEW ARNOLD

Come, dear children, let us away;
Down and away below!
Now my brothers call from the bay,
Now the great winds shoreward blow,
Now the salt tides seaward flow;
Now the wild white horses play,
Champ and chafe and toss in the spray.
Children dear, let us away!
This way, this way!

Call her once before you go –
Call once yet!
In a voice that she will know:
'Margaret! Margaret!'
Children's voices should be dear
(Call once more) to a mother's ear;
Children's voices, wild with pain –
Surely she will come again!
Call her once and come away;
This way, this way!
'Mother dear, we cannot stay!
The wild white horses foam and fret.'
Margaret! Margaret!

Come, dear children, come away down;
Call no more!
One last look at the white wall'd town,
And the little grey church on the windy shore;
Then come down!

She will not come though you call all day;
Come away, come away!

Children dear, was it yesterday
We heard the sweet bells over the bay?
In the caverns where we lay,
Through the surf and through the swell,
The far-off sound of a silver bell?
Sand-strewn caverns, cool and deep,
Where the winds are all asleep;
Where the spent lights quiver and gleam,
Where the salt weed sways in the stream,
Where the sea-beasts, ranged all round,
Feed in the ooze of their pasture-ground;
Where the sea-snakes coil and twine,
Dry their mail and bask in the brine;
Where great whales come sailing by,
Sail and sail, with unshut eye,
Round the world for ever and aye?
When did music come this way?
Children dear, was it yesterday?
Children dear, was it yesterday?
(Call yet once) that she went away?
Once she sate with you and me,
On the red gold throne in the heart of the sea,
And the youngest sate on her knee.
She comb'd its bright hair, and she tended it well,
When down swung the sound of a far-off bell.
She sigh'd, she look'd up through the clear green sea;
She said: 'I must go, for my kinsfolk pray
In the little grey church on the shore to-day.
'Twill be Easter-time in the world – ah me!
And I lose my poor soul, Merman! here with thee.
I said: 'Go up, dear heart, through the waves;

Say thy prayer, and come back to the kind sea-caves.
She smiled, she went up through the surf in the bay.
Children dear, was it yesterday?

  Children dear, were we long alone?
'The sea grows stormy, the little ones moan;
Long prayers,' I said, 'in the world they say;
Come!' I said; and we rose through the surf in the bay
We went up the beach, by the sandy down
Where the sea-stocks bloom, to the white-wall'd town
Through the narrow paved streets, where all was still,
To the little grey church on the windy hill.
From the church came a murmur of folk at their
  prayers
But we stood without in the cold blowing airs.
We climb'd on the graves, on the stones worn with
  rains
And we gazed up the aisle through the small leaded
  panes
She sate by the pillar; we saw her clear:
'Margaret, hist! come quick, we are here!
Dear heart,' I said, 'we are long alone;
The sea grows stormy, the little ones moan.'
But, ah, she gave me never a look,
For her eyes were seal'd to the holy book!
Loud prays the priest; shut stands the door.
Come away, children, call no more!
Come away, come down, call no more!

  Down, down, down!
Down to the depths of the sea!
She sits at her wheel in the humming town,
Singing most joyfully.
Hark what she sings: 'O joy, O joy,

For the humming street, and the child with its toy!
For the priest, and the bell, and the holy well;
For the wheel where I spun,
And the blessed light of the sun!'
And so she sings her fill,
Singing most joyfully,
Till the spindle drops from her hand,
And the whizzing wheel stands still.
She steals to the window, and looks at the sand,
And over the sand at the sea;
And her eyes are set in a stare;
And anon there breaks a sigh,
And anon there drops a tear,
From a sorrow-clouded eye,
And a heart sorrow-laden,
A long, long sigh;
For the cold strange eyes of a little Mermaiden
And the gleam of her golden hair.

  Come away, away children;
Come children, come down!
The hoarse wind blows coldly;
Lights shine in the town
She will start from her slumber
When gusts shake the door;
She will hear the winds howling,
Will hear the waves roar.
We shall see, while above us
The waves roar and whirl,
A ceiling of amber,
A pavement of pearl.
Singing: 'Here came a mortal,
But faithless was she!

And alone dwell for ever
The kings of the sea.'

But, children, at midnight,
When soft the winds blow,
When clear falls the moonlight,
When spring-tides are low;
When sweet airs come seaward
From heaths starr'd with broom,
And high rocks throw mildly
On the blanch'd sands a gloom;
Up the still, glistening beaches,
Up the creeks we will hie,
Over banks of bright seaweed
The ebb-tide leaves dry.
We will gaze, from the sand-hills,
At the white, sleeping town;
At the church on the hill-side –
And then come back down.
Singing: 'There dwells a loved one,
But cruel is she!
She left lonely for ever
The kings of the sea.'

If I Could Tell You

W. H. AUDEN

Time will say nothing but I told you so,
Time only knows the price we have to pay;
If I could tell you I would let you know.

If we should weep when clowns put on their show,
If we should stumble when musicians play,
Time will say nothing but I told you so.

There are no fortunes to be told, although,
Because I love you more than I can say,
If I could tell you I would let you know.

The winds must come from somewhere when they
  blow,
There must be reasons why the leaves decay;
Time will say nothing but I told you so.

Perhaps the roses really want to grow,
The vision seriously intends to stay;
If I could tell you I would let you know.

Suppose the lions all get up and go,
And all the brooks and soldiers run away;
Will Time say nothing but I told you so?
If I could tell you I would let you know.

Going Down Hill On A Bicycle: A Boy's Song

HENRY CHARLES BEECHING

With lifted feet, hands still,
I am poised, and down the hill
Dart, with heedful mind;
The air goes by in a wind.

Swifter and yet more swift,
Till the heart with a mighty lift
Makes the lungs laugh, the throat cry:–
'O bird, see; see, bird, I fly.

'Is this, is this your joy?
O bird, then I, though a boy,
For a golden moment share
Your feathery life in air!'

Say, heart, is there aught like this
In a world that is full of bliss?
'Tis more than skating, bound
Steel-shod to the level ground.

Speed slackens now, I float
Awhile in my airy boat;
Till, when the wheels scarce crawl,
My feet to the treadles fall.

Alas, that the longest hill
Must end in a vale; but still,
Who climbs with toil, wheresoe'er,
Shall find wings waiting there.

Which Shall It Be?

ETHEL LYNN BEERS

'Which shall it be? Which shall it be?'
I look'd at John – John look'd at me
(Dear, patient John, who loves me yet
As well as though my locks were jet);
And when I found that I must speak,
My voice seemed strangely low and weak:
'Tell me again what Robert said.'
And then I, listening, bent my head.
'This is his letter: "I will give
A house and land while you shall live,
If, in return, from out your seven,
One child to me for aye is given."'
I looked at John's old garments worn,
I thought of all that John had borne
Of poverty and work and care,
Which I, though willing, could not share;
I thought of seven mouths to feed,
Of seven little children's need,
And then of this. 'Come, John,' said I,
'We'll choose among them as they lie
Asleep;' so, walking hand in hand,
Dear John and I surveyed our band.
First to the cradle lightly stepped,
Where the new nameless baby slept.
'Shall it be Baby?' whispered John.
I took his hand, and hurried on
To Lily's crib. Her sleeping grasp
Held her old doll within its clasp;
Her dark curls lay like gold alight,

A glory 'gainst the pillow white.
Softly her father stoop'd to lay
His rough hand down in loving way,
When dream or whisper made her stir,
Then huskily said John, 'Not her, not her!'
We stopp'd beside the trundle bed,
And one long ray of lamplight shed
Athwart the boyish faces there,
In sleep so pitiful and fair;
I saw on Jamie's rough, red cheek
A tear undried. Ere John could speak,
'He's but a baby, too,' said I,
And kiss'd him as we hurried by.
Pale, patient Robbie's angel face
Still in his sleep bore suffering's trace.
'No, for a thousand crowns, not him!'
We whisper'd, while our eyes were dim.
Poor Dick! bad Dick! our wayward son,
Turbulent, reckless, idle one –
Could he be spared? Nay; He who gave
Bids us befriend him to his grave;
Only a mother's heart can be
Patient enough for such as he;
'And so,' said John, 'I would not dare
To send him from her bedside prayer.'
Then stole we softly up above
And knelt by Mary, child of love.
'Perhaps for her 'twould better be,'
I said to John. Quite silently
He lifted up a curl astray
Across her cheek in wilful way,
And shook his head: 'Nay, love; not thee,'
The while my heart beat audibly.
Only one more, our eldest lad,

Trusty and truthful, good and glad –
So like his father. 'No, John, no –
I cannot, will not, let him go.'
And so we wrote, in courteous way,
We could not give one child away;
And afterward toil lighter seemed,
Thinking of that of which we dreamed,
Happy in truth that not one face
We missed from its accustomed place;
Thankful to work for all the seven,
Trusting the rest to One in heaven.

Tarantella

HILAIRE BELLOC

Do you remember an Inn,
Miranda?
Do you remember an Inn?
And the tedding and the spreading
Of the straw for a bedding,
And the fleas that tease in the High Pyrenees,
And the wine that tasted of the tar?
And the cheers and the jeers of the young muleteers
(Under the vine of the dark verandah)?
Do you remember an Inn, Miranda,
Do you remember an Inn?
And the cheers and the jeers of the young muleteers
Who hadn't got a penny,
And who weren't paying any,
And the hammer at the doors and the Din?
And the Hip! Hop! Hap!
Of the clap
Of the hands to the twirl and the swirl
Of the girl gone chancing,
Glancing,
Dancing,
Backing and advancing,
Snapping of a clapper to the spin
Out and in —
And the Ting, Tong, Tang of the Guitar!
Do you remember an Inn,
Miranda?
Do you remember an Inn?

Never more;
Miranda,
Never more.
Only the high peaks hoar:
And Aragon a torrent at the door.
No sound
In the walls of the Halls where falls
The tread
Of the feet of the dead to the ground
No sound:
But the boom
Of the far Waterfall like Doom.

Diary Of A Church Mouse

JOHN BETJEMAN

Here among long-discarded cassocks,
Damp stools, and half-split open hassocks,
Here where the Vicar never looks
I nibble through old service books.
Lean and alone I spend my days
Behind this Church of England baize.
I share my dark forgotten room
With two oil-lamps and half a broom.
The cleaner never bothers me,
So here I eat my frugal tea.
My bread is sawdust mixed with straw;
My jam is polish for the floor.
  Christmas and Easter may be feasts
For congregations and for priests,
And so may Whitsun. All the same,
They do not fill my meagre frame.
For me the only feast at all
Is Autumn's Harvest Festival,
When I can satisfy my want
With ears of corn around the font.
I climb the eagle's brazen head
To burrow through a loaf of bread.
I scramble up the pulpit stair
And gnaw the marrows hanging there.
  It is enjoyable to taste
These items ere they go to waste,
But how annoying when one finds
That other mice with pagan minds
Come into church my food to share

Who have no proper business there.
Two field mice who have no desire
To be baptized, invade the choir.
A large and most unfriendly rat
Comes in to see what we are at.
He says he thinks there is no God
And yet he comes ... it's rather odd.
This year he stole a sheaf of wheat
(It screened our special preacher's seat),
And prosperous mice from fields away
Come in to hear the organ play,
And under cover of its notes
Eat through the altar's sheaf of oats.
A Low Church mouse, who thinks that I
Am too papistical, and High,
Yet somehow doesn't think it wrong
To munch through Harvest Evensong,
While I, who starve the whole year through,
Must share my food with rodents who
Except at this time of the year
Not once inside the church appear.
  Within the human world I know
Such goings-on could not be so,
For human beings only do
What their religion tells them to.
They read the Bible every day
And always, night and morning, pray,
And just like me, the good church mouse,
Worship each week in God's own house.
  But all the same it's strange to me
How very full the church can be
With people I don't see at all
Except at Harvest Festival.

The Little Black Boy

WILLIAM BLAKE

My mother bore me in the southern wild,
  And I am black, but O! my soul is white!
White as an angel is the English child,
  But I am black, as if bereav'd of light.

My mother taught me underneath a tree,
  And sitting down before the heat of day
She took me on her lap and kissed me,
  And pointing to the east began to say:

'Look on the rising sun: there God does live,
  And gives his light, and gives his heat away,
And flowers and trees and beasts and men receive
  Comfort in morning, joy in the noon day.

'And we are put on earth a little space,
  That we may learn to bear the beams of love;
And these black bodies and this sun-burnt face
  Is but a cloud, and like a shady grove.

'For when our souls have learn'd the heat to bear,
  The cloud will vanish; we shall hear his voice,
Saying: "Come out from the grove, my love & care,
  And round my golden tent like lambs rejoice." '

Thus did my mother say, and kissed me,
  And thus I say to little English boy:
When I from black and he from white cloud free,
  And round the tent of God like lambs we joy,

I'll shade him from the heat, till he can bear
  To lean in joy upon our father's knee;
And then I'll stand and stroke his silver hair,
  And be like him, and he will then love me.

Farewell

ANNE BRONTË

Farewell to Thee! But not farewell
To all my fondest thoughts of Thee;
Within my heart they still shall dwell
And they shall cheer and comfort me.

Life seems more sweet that Thou didst live
And men more true that Thou wert one;
Nothing is lost that Thou didst give,
Nothing destroyed that Thou hast done.

The Old Vicarage, Grantchester

(*Café des Westens*, Berlin, May 1912)

RUPERT BROOKE

Just now the lilac is in bloom,
All before my little room;
And in my flower-beds, I think,
Smile the carnation and the pink;
And down the borders, well I know,
The poppy and the pansy blow . . .
Oh! there the chestnuts, summer through,
Beside the river make for you
A tunnel of green gloom, and sleep
Deeply above; and green and deep
The stream mysterious glides beneath,
Green as a dream and deep as death.
– Oh, damn! I know it! and I know
How the May fields all golden show,
And when the day is young and sweet,
Gild gloriously the bare feet.
That run to bathe . . .

> *Du lieber Gott!*

Here am I, sweating, sick, and hot,
And there the shadowed waters fresh
Lean up to embrace the naked flesh.
Temperamentvoll German Jews
Drink beer around – and *there* the dews
Are soft beneath a morn of gold.
Here tulips bloom as they are told;
Unkempt about those hedges blows
An English unofficial rose;

And there the unregulated sun
Slopes down to rest when day is done,
And wakes a vague unpunctual star,
A slippered Hesper; and there are
Meads towards Haslingfield and Coton
Where *das Betreten's* not *verboten*.

E᾿ίθε γενοίμην . . . would I were
In Grantchester, in Grantchester!
Some, it may be, can get in touch
With Nature there, or Earth, or such.
And clever modern men have seen
A Faun a-peeping through the green,
And felt the Classics were not dead,
To glimpse a Naiad's reedy head,
Or hear the Goat-foot piping low: . . .
But these are things I do not know.
I only know that you may lie
Day-long and watch the Cambridge sky,
And, flower-lulled in sleepy grass,
Hear the cool lapse of hours pass,
Until the centuries blend and blur
In Grantchester, in Grantchester . . .
Still in the dawnlit waters cool
His ghostly Lordship swims his pool,
And tries the strokes, essays the tricks,
Long learnt on Hellespont, or Styx.
Dan Chaucer hears his river still
Chatter beneath a phantom mill.

Tennyson notes, with studious eye,
How Cambridge waters hurry by . . .
And in that garden, black and white,
Creep whispers through the grass all night;

And spectral dance, before the dawn,
A hundred Vicars down the lawn;
Curates, long dust, will come and go
On lissom, clerical, printless toe;
And oft between the boughs is seen
The sly shade of a Rural Dean . . .
Till, at a shiver in the skies,
Vanishing with Satanic cries,
The prim ecclesiastic rout
Leaves but a startled sleeper-out,
Grey heavens, the first bird's drowsy calls,
The falling house that never falls.

God! I will pack, and take a train,
And get me to England once again!
For England's the one land, I know,
Where men with Splendid Hearts may go;
And Cambridgeshire, of all England,
The shire for Men who Understand;
And of *that* district I prefer
The lovely hamlet Grantchester.
For Cambridge people rarely smile,
Being urban, squat, and packed with guile;
And Royston men in the far South
Are black and fierce and strange of mouth;
At Over they fling oaths at one,
And worse than oaths at Trumpington,
And Ditton girls are mean and dirty,
And there's none in Harston under thirty,
And folks in Shelford and those parts
Have twisted lips and twisted hearts,
And Barton men make Cockney rhymes,
And Coton's full of nameless crimes,
And things are done you'd not believe

At Madingley, on Christmas Eve.
Strong men have run for miles and miles,
When one from Cherry Hinton smiles;
Strong men have blanched, and shot their wives,
Rather than send them to St Ives;
Strong men have cried like babies, bydam,
To hear what happened at Babraham.
But Grantchester! ah, Grantchester!
There's peace and holy quiet there,
Great clouds along pacific skies,
And men and women with straight eyes,
Lithe children lovelier than a dream,
A bosky wood, a slumbrous stream,
And little kindly winds that creep
Round twilight corners, half asleep.
In Grantchester their skins are white;
They bathe by day, they bathe by night;
The women there do all they ought;
The men observe the Rules of Thought.
They love the Good; they worship Truth;
They laugh uproariously in youth;
(And when they get to feeling old,
They up and shoot themselves, I'm told) . . .

  Ah God! to see the branches stir
Across the moon at Grantchester!
To smell the thrilling-sweet and rotten
Unforgettable, unforgotten
River-smell, and hear the breeze
Sobbing in the little trees.
Say, do the elm-clumps greatly stand
Still guardians of that holy land?
The chestnuts shade, in reverend dream,
The yet unacademic stream?

Is dawn a secret shy and cold
Anadyomene, silver-gold?
And sunset still a golden sea
From Haslingfield to Madingley?
And after, ere the night is born,
Do hares come out about the corn?
Oh, is the water sweet and cool,
Gentle and brown, above the pool?
And laughs the immortal river still
Under the mill, under the mill?
Say, is there Beauty yet to find?
And Certainty? and Quiet kind?
Deep meadows yet, for to forget
The lies, and truths, and pain? . . . oh! yet
Stands the Church clock at ten to three?
And is there honey still for tea?

Prospice

ROBERT BROWNING

Fear death? – to feel the fog in my throat,
  The mist in my face,
When the snows begin, and the blasts denote
  I am nearing the place,
The power of the night, the press of the storm,
  The post of the foe;
Where he stands, the Arch Fear in a visible form,
  Yet the strong man must go:
For the journey is done and the summit attained,
  And the barriers fall,
Though a battle's to fight ere the guerdon be gained,
  The reward of it all.
I was ever a fighter, so – one fight more,
  The best and the last!
I would hate that death bandaged my eyes, and
    forbore,
  And bade me creep past.
No! let me taste the whole of it, fare like my peers
  The heroes of old,
Bear the brunt, in a minute pay glad life's arrears
  Of pain, darkness and cold.
For sudden the worst turns the best to the brave,
  The black minute's at end,
And the elements' rage, the fiend-voices that rave,
  Shall dwindle, shall blend,
Shall change, shall become first a peace out of pain,
  Then a light, then thy breast,
O thou soul of my soul! I shall clasp thee again,
  And with God be the rest!

A Song Of Living

AMELIA JOSEPHINE BURR

Because I have loved life, I shall have no sorrow to die.
I have sent up my gladness on wings, to be lost in the
blue of the sky.
I have run and leaped with the rain, I have taken the
wind to my breast.
My cheek like a drowsy child to the face of the earth I
have pressed.
Because I have loved life, I shall have no sorrow to die.

I have kissed young Love on the lips, I have heard his
song to the end.
I have struck my hand like a seal in the loyal hand of
a friend.
I have known the peace of heaven, the comfort of
work done well.
I have longed for death in the darkness and risen alive
out of hell.
Because I have loved life, I shall have no sorrow to die.

I give a share of my soul to the world where my
course is run.
I know that another shall finish the task I must leave
undone.
I know that no flower, nor flint was in vain on the
path I trod.
As one looks on a face through a window, through life
I have looked on God.
Because I have loved life, I shall have no sorrow to die.

Timothy Winters

CHARLES CAUSLEY

Timothy Winters comes to school
With eyes as wide as a football-pool,
Ears like bombs and teeth like splinters:
A blitz of a boy is Timothy Winters.

His belly is white, his neck is dark,
And his hair is an exclamation-mark.
His clothes are enough to scare a crow
And through his britches the blue winds blow.

When teacher talks he won't hear a word
And he shoots down dead the arithmetic-bird,
He licks the patterns off his plate
And he's not even heard of the Welfare State.

Timothy Winters has bloody feet
And he lives in a house on Suez Street,
He sleeps in a sack on the kitchen floor
And they say there aren't boys like him any more.

Old Man Winters likes his beer
And his missus ran off with a bombardier,
Grandma sits in the grate with a gin
And Timothy's dosed with an aspirin.

The Welfare Worker lies awake
But the law's as tricky as a ten-foot snake,
So Timothy Winters drinks his cup
And slowly goes on growing up.

At Morning Prayers the Master helves
For children less fortunate than ourselves,
And the loudest response in the room is when
Timothy Winters roars 'Amen!'

So come one angel, come on ten:
Timothy Winters says 'Amen
Amen amen amen amen.'
Timothy Winters, Lord.

                    Amen.

Morning

JOHN CLARE

The morning comes, the drops of dew
Hang on the grass and bushes too;
The sheep more eager bite the grass
Whose moisture gleams like drops of glass;
The heifer licks in grass and dew
That make her drink and fodder too.
The little bird his morn-song gives,
His breast wet with the dripping leaves,
Then stops abruptly just to fly
And catch the wakened butterfly,
That goes to sleep behind the flowers
Or backs of leaves from dews and showers.
The yellow-hammer, haply blest,
Sits by the dyke upon her nest;
The long grass hides her from the day,
The water keeps the boys away.
The morning sun is round and red
As crimson curtains round a bed,
The dewdrops hang on barley horns
As beads the necklace thread adorns,
The dewdrops hang wheat-ears upon
Like golden drops against the sun.
Hedge-sparrows in the bush cry 'tweet',
O'er nests larks winnow in the wheat,
Till the sun turns gold and gets more high,
And paths are clean and grass gets dry,
And longest shadows pass away.
And brightness is the blaze of day.

Say Not The Struggle Naught Availeth

ARTHUR HUGH CLOUGH

Say not the struggle naught availeth,
    The labour and the wounds are vain,
The enemy faints not, nor faileth,
    And as things have been, things remain.

If hopes were dupes, fears may be liars;
    It may be, in yon smoke concealed,
Your comrades chase e'en now the fliers,
    And, but for you, possess the field.

For while the tired waves, vainly breaking,
    Seem here no painful inch to gain,
Far back through creeks and inlets making
    Comes silent, flooding in, the main.

And not by eastern windows only,
    When daylight comes, comes in the light;
In front the sun climbs slow, how slowly,
    But westward, look, the land is bright!

An Old Woman Of The Roads

PADRAIC COLUM

O, to have a little house!
To own the hearth and stool and all!
The heaped-up sods upon the fire,
The pile of turf against the wall!

To have a clock with weights and chains
And pendulum swinging up and down,
A dresser filled with shining delph,
Speckled and white and blue and brown!

I could be busy all the day
Clearing and sweeping hearth and floor,
And fixing on their shelf again
My white and blue and speckled store!

I could be quiet there at night
Beside the fire and by myself,
Sure of a bed and loth to leave
The ticking clock and shining delph!

Och! but I'm weary of mist and dark,
And roads where there's never a house or bush,
And tired I am of bog and road,
And the crying wind and the lonesome hush!

And I am praying to God on high,
And I am praying Him night and day,
For a little house, a house of my own –
Out of the wind's and the rain's way.

The Crowning Of Dreaming John Of Grafton

JOHN DRINKWATER

I

Seven days he travelled
Down the roads of England,
Out of leafy Warwick lanes
Into London Town.
Grey and very wrinkled
Was Dreaming John of Grafton,
But seven days he walked to see
A king put on his crown.

Down the streets of London
He asked the crowded people
Where would be the crowning
And when would it begin.
He said he'd got a shilling,
A shining silver shilling,
But when he came to Westminster
They wouldn't let him in.

Dreaming John of Grafton
Looked upon the people,
Laughed a little laugh, and then
Whistled and was gone.
Out along the long roads,
The twisting roads of England,
Back into the Warwick lanes
Wandered Dreaming John.

2

As twilight touched with her ghostly fingers
All the meadows and mellow hills,
And the great sun swept in his robes of glory –
Woven of petals of daffodils
And jewelled and fringed with leaves of the roses –
Down the plains of the western way,
Among the rows of the scented clover
Dreaming John in his dreaming lay.

Since dawn had folded the stars of heaven
He'd counted a score of miles and five,
And now, with a vagabond heart untroubled
And proud as the properest man alive,
He sat him down with a limber spirit
That all men covet and few may keep,
And he watched the summer draw round her beauty
The shadow that shepherds the world to sleep.

And up from the valleys and shining rivers,
And out of the shadowy wood-ways wild,
And down from the secret hills, and streaming
Out of the shimmering undefiled
Wonder of sky that arched him over,
Came a company shod in gold
And girt in gowns of a thousand blossoms,
Laughing and rainbow-aureoled.

Wrinkled and grey and with eyes a-wonder
And soul beatified, Dreaming John
Watched the marvellous company gather
While over the clover a glory shone;
They bore on their brows the hues of heaven,

Their limbs were sweet with flowers of the fields,
And their feet were bright with the gleaming treasure
That prodigal earth to her children yields.

They stood before him, and John was laughing
As they were laughing; he knew them all,
Spirits of trees and pools and meadows,
Mountain and windy waterfall,
Spirits of clouds and skies and rivers,
Leaves and shadows and rain and sun,
A crowded, jostling, laughing army,
And Dreaming John knew every one.

Among them then was a sound of singing
And chiming music, as one came down
The level rows of the scented clover,
Bearing aloft a flashing crown;
No word of a man's desert was spoken,
Nor any word of a man's unworth,
But there on the wrinkled brow it rested,
And Dreaming John was king of the earth.

3

Dreaming John of Grafton
Went away to London,
Saw the coloured banners fly,
Heard the great bells ring,
But though his tongue was civil
And he had a silver shilling,
They wouldn't let him in to see
The crowning of the King.

So back along the long roads,
The leafy roads of England,
Dreaming John went carolling,
Travelling alone,
And in a summer evening,
Among the scented clover,
He held before a shouting throng
A crowning of his own.

My Mind To Me A Kingdom Is

SIR EDWARD DYER

My mind to me a kingdom is;
  Such present joys therein I find,
That it excels all other bliss
  That world affords or grows by kind.
Though much I want which most would have
Yet still my mind forbids to crave.

No princely pomp, no wealthy store,
  No force to win the victory,
No wily wit to salve a sore,
  No shape to feed a loving eye;
To none of these I yield as thrall,
For why, my mind doth serve for all.

I see how plenty suffers oft,
  And hasty climbers soon do fall;
I see that those which are aloft
  Mishap doth threaten most of all.
They get with toil, they keep with fear;
Such cares my mind could never bear.

Content I live, this is my stay,
  I seek no more than may suffice;
I press to bear no haughty sway;
  Look, what I lack my mind supplies.
Lo! thus I triumph like a king,
Content with that my mind doth bring.

Some have too much, yet still do crave;
  I little have, and seek no more.
They are but poor, though much they have,
  And I am rich with little store.
They poor, I rich; they beg, I give;
They lack, I leave; they pine, I live.

I laugh not at another's loss,
  I grudge not at another's gain;
No wordly waves my mind can toss;
  My state at one doth still remain.
I fear no foe, I fawn no friend;
I loathe not life, nor dread my end.

Some weigh their pleasure by their lust,
  Their wisdom by their rage of will;
Their treasure is their only trust,
  A cloaked craft their store of skill.
But all the pleasure that I find
Is to maintain a quiet mind.

My wealth is health and perfect ease;
  My conscience clear my choice defence;
I neither seek by bribes to please
  Nor by deceit to breed offence.
Thus do I live, thus will I die;
Would all did so as well as I!

Desiderata

MAX EHRMANN

'Go placidly amid the noise and the haste, and remember what peace there may be in silence. As far as possible without surrender be on good terms with all persons. Speak your truth quietly and clearly; and listen to others, even the dull and ignorant; they too have their story. Avoid loud and aggressive persons, they are vexatious to the spirit. If you compare yourself with others you may become vain and bitter; for always there will be greater and lesser persons than yourself. Enjoy your achievements as well as your plans. Keep interested in your own career, however humble; it is a real possession in the changing fortunes of time. Exercise caution in your business affairs; for the world is full of trickery. But let this not blind you to what virtue there is; many persons strive for high ideals; and everywhere life is full of heroism. Be yourself. Especially do not feign affection. Neither be cynical about love; for in the face of all aridity and disenchantment it is as perennial as the grass. Take kindly the counsel of the years, gracefully surrendering the things of youth. Nurture strength of spirit to shield you in sudden misfortune. But do not distress yourself with imaginings. Many fears are born of fatigue and loneliness. Beyond a wholesome discipline, be gentle with yourself. You are a child of the universe no less than the trees and the stars; you have a right to be here. And whether or not it is clear to you, no doubt the universe is unfolding as it should. Therefore be at peace with God, whatever you conceive Him to be. And whatever your labors and aspirations, in the noisy confusion of life keep peace with your soul. With all its sham, drudgery and broken dreams, it is still a beautiful world. Be cheerful. Strive to be happy.'

Mrs Malone

ELEANOR FARJEON

Mrs Malone
Lived hard by a wood
All on her lonesome
As nobody should.
With her crust on a plate
And her pot on the coal
And none but herself
To converse with, poor soul.
In a shawl and a hood
She got sticks out-o'door,
On a bit of old sacking
She slept on the floor,
And nobody nobody
Asked how she fared
Or knew how she managed,
For nobody cared.
Why make a pother
About an old crone?
What for should they bother
With Mrs Malone?

One Monday in winter
With snow on the ground
So thick that a footstep
Fell without sound,
She heard a faint frostbitten
Peck on the pane
And went to the window
To listen again.

There sat a cock-sparrow
Bedraggled and weak,
With half-open eyelid
And ice on his beak.
She threw up the sash
And she took the bird in,
And mumbled and fumbled it
Under her chin.

 'Ye're all of a smother,
 Ye're fair overblown!
 I've room fer another,'
 Said Mrs Malone.

Come Tuesday while eating
Her dry morning slice
With the sparrow a-picking
('Ain't company nice!')
She heard on her doorpost
A curious scratch,
And there was a cat
With its claw on the latch.
It was hungry and thirsty
And thin as a lath,
It mewed and it mowed
On the slithery path.
She threw the door open
And warmed up some pap,
And huddled and cuddled it
In her old lap.

 'There, there, little brother,
 Ye poor skin-an'-bone,
 There's room fer another,'
 Said Mrs Malone.

Come Wednesday while all of them
Crouched on the mat
With a crumb for the sparrow,
A sip for the cat,
There was a wailing and whining
Outside in the wood,
And there sat a vixen
With six of her brood.
She was haggard and ragged
And worn to a shred,
And her half-dozen babies
Were only half-fed,
But Mrs Malone, crying
'My! ain't they sweet!'
Happed them and lapped them
And gave them to eat.
        'You warm yerself, mother,
        Ye're cold as a stone!
        There's room fer another,'
        Said Mrs Malone.

Come Thursday a donkey
Stepped in off the road
With sores on his withers
From bearing a load.
Come Friday when icicles
Pierced the white air
Down from the mountainside
Lumbered a bear.
For each she had something,
If little, to give –
'Lord knows, the poor critters
Must all of 'em live,'
She gave them her sacking,

Her hood and her shawl,
Her loaf and her teapot –
She gave them her all.
    'What with one thing and t'other
    Me fambily's grown,
    And there's room fer another,'
    Said Mrs Malone.

Come Saturday evening
When time was to sup
Mrs Malone
Had forgot to sit up.
The cat said meeow,
And the sparrow said peep,
The vixen, she's sleeping,
The bear, let her sleep.
On the back of the donkey
They bore her away,
Through trees and up mountains
Beyond night and day,
Till come Sunday morning
They brought her in state
Through the last cloudbank
As far as the Gate.
    'Who is it,' asked Peter,
    'You have with you there?'
    And donkey and sparrow,
    Cat, vixen, and bear

Exclaimed, 'Do you tell us
Up here she's unknown?
It's our mother, God bless us!
It's Mrs Malone,
Whose havings were few

nd whose holding was small
nd whose heart was so big
: had room for us all.'
'hen Mrs Malone
)f a sudden awoke,
he rubbed her two eyeballs
nd anxiously spoke:
Where am I, to goodness,
nd what do I see?
/Iy dear, let's turn back,
'his ain't no place for me!'
ut Peter said, 'Mother
;o in to the Throne.
'here's room for another
)ne, Mrs Malone.'

from The Rubáiyát Of Omar Khayyám Of Naishápúr

EDWARD FITZGERALD

Here with a Loaf of Bread beneath the Bough,
A Flask of Wine, a Book of Verse – and Thou
  Beside me singing in the Wilderness –
And Wilderness is Paradise enow.

'How sweet is mortal Sovranty' – think some:
Others – 'How blest the Paradise to come!'
  Ah, take the Cash in hand and waive the Rest;
Oh, the brave Music of a distant Drum!

Look to the Rose that blows about us – 'Lo,
Laughing,' she says, 'into the World I blow:
  At once the silken Tassel of my Purse
Tear, and its Treasure on the Garden throw.'

The Worldly Hope men set their Hearts upon
Turns Ashes – or it prospers; and anon,
  Like Snow upon the Desert's dusty Face
Lighting a little Hour or two – is gone.

And those who husbanded the Golden Grain,
And those who flung it to the Winds like Rain,
  Alike to no such aureate Earth are turn'd
As, buried once, Men want dug up again.

Think, in this batter'd Caravanserai
Whose Doorways are alternate Night and Day,
  How Sultán after Sultán with his Pomp
Abode his Hour or two, and went his way.

They say the Lion and the Lizard keep
The Courts where Jamshyd gloried and drank deep;
  And Bahrám, that great Hunter – the Wild Ass
Stamps o'er his Head, and he lies fast asleep.

I sometimes think that never blows so red
The Rose as where some buried Caesar bled;
  That every Hyacinth the Garden wears
Dropt in its Lap from some once lovely Head.

And this delightful Herb whose tender Green
Fledges the River's Lip on which we lean –
  Ah, lean upon it lightly! for who knows
From what once lovely Lip it springs unseen!

Ah, my Belovèd, fill the Cup that clears
TO-DAY of past Regrets and future Fears –
  To-morrow? – Why, To-morrow I may be
Myself with Yesterday's Sev'n Thousand Years.

Lo! some we loved, the loveliest and best
That Time and Fate of all their Vintage prest,
  Have drunk their Cup a Round or two before,
And one by one crept silently to Rest.

And we, that now make merry in the Room
They left, and Summer dresses in new Bloom,
  Ourselves must we beneath the Couch of Earth
Descend, ourselves to make a Couch – for whom?

Ah, make the most of what we yet may spend,
Before we too into the Dust descend;
  Dust into Dust, and under Dust, to lie,
Sans Wine, sans Song, sans Singer, and – sans End!

Brumana

JAMES ELROY FLECKER

Oh shall I never never be home again?
Meadows of England shining in the rain
Spread wide your daisied lawns: your ramparts green
With briar fortify, with blossom screen
Till my far morning – and O streams that slow
And pure and deep through plains and playlands go,
For me your love and all your kingcups store,
And – dark militia of the southern shore,
Old fragrant friends – preserve me the last lines
Of that long saga which you sung me, pines,
When, lonely boy, beneath the chosen tree
I listened, with my eyes upon the sea.

O traitor pines, you sang what life has found
The falsest of fair tales.
Earth blew a far-horn prelude all around,
That native music of her forest home,
While from the sea's blue fields and syren dales
Shadows and light noon-spectres of the foam
Riding the summer gales
On aery viols plucked an idle sound.

Hearing you sing, O trees,
Hearing you murmur, 'There are older seas,
That beat on vaster sands,
Where the wise snailfish move their pearly towers
To carven rocks and sculptured promont'ries,'
Hearing you whisper, 'Lands
Where blaze the unimaginable flowers.'

Beneath me in the valley waves the palm,
Beneath, beyond the valley, breaks the sea;
Beneath me sleep in mist and light and calm
Cities of Lebanon, dream-shadow-dim,
Where Kings of Tyre and Kings of Tyre did rule
In ancient days in endless dynasty.
And all around the snowy mountains swim
Like mighty swans afloat in heaven's pool.

But I will walk upon the wooded hill
Where stands a grove, O pines, of sister pines,
And when the downy twilight droops her wing
And no sea glimmers and no mountain shines
My heart shall listen still.
For pines are gossip pines the wide world through
And full of runic tales to sigh or sing.
'Tis ever sweet through pines to see the sky
Mantling a deeper gold or darker blue.

'Tis ever sweet to lie
On the dry carpet of the needles brown,
And though the fanciful green lizard stir
And windy odours light as thistledown
Breathe from the lavdanon and lavender,
Half to forget the wandering and pain,
Half to remember days that have gone by,
And dream and dream that I am home again!

The Ice Cart

WILFRID WILSON GIBSON

Perched on my city office-stool
I watched with envy while a cool
And lucky carter handled ice . . .
And I was wandering in a trice
Far from the grey and grimy heat
Of that intolerable street
O'er sapphire berg and emerald floe
Beneath the still cold ruby glow
Of everlasting Polar night,
Bewildered by the queer half-light,
Until I stumbled unawares
Upon a creek where big white bears
Plunged headlong down with flourished heels
And floundered after shining seals
Through shivering seas of blinding blue.
And, as I watched them, ere I knew
I'd stripped and I was swimming too
Among the seal-pack, young and hale,
And thrusting on with threshing tail,
With twist and twirl and sudden leap
Through crackling ice and salty deep,
Diving and doubling with my kind,
Until, at last, we left behind
Those big white, blundering bulks of death,
And lay, at length, with panting breath
Upon a far untravelled floe,
Beneath a gentle drift of snow –
Snow drifting gently, fine and white,
Out of the endless Polar night,

Falling and falling evermore
Upon that far untravelled shore,
Till I was buried fathoms deep
Beneath that cold, white drifting sleep –
Sleep drifting deep,
Deep drifting sleep . . .
The carter cracked a sudden whip:
I clutched my stool with startled grip,
Awakening to the grimy heat
Of that intolerable street.

from The Deserted Village

OLIVER GOLDSMITH

Beside yon straggling fence that skirts the way,
With blossomed furze unprofitably gay,
There, in his noisy mansion, skilled to rule,
The village master taught his little school;
A man severe he was, and stern to view;
I knew him well, and every truant knew;
Well had the boding tremblers learned to trace
The day's disasters in his morning face;
Full well they laughed, with counterfeited glee,
At all his jokes, for many a joke had he;
Full well the busy whisper, circling round,
Conveyed the dismal tidings when he frowned;
Yet he was kind, or, if severe in aught,
The love he bore to learning was in fault;
The village all declared how much he knew;
'Twas certain he could write, and cipher too;
Lands he could measure, terms and tides presage,
And e'en the story ran that he could gauge.
In arguing too, the parson owned his skill,
For e'en though vanquished, he could argue still;
While words of learned length and thundering sound
Amazed the gazing rustics ranged around,
And still they gazed, and still the wonder grew,
That one small head could carry all he knew.

Elegy Written In
A Country Churchyard

THOMAS GRAY

The curfew tolls the knell of parting day,
  The lowing herd wind slowly o'er the lea,
The plowman homeward plods his weary way,
  And leaves the world to darkness and to me.

Now fades the glimmering landscape on the sight,
  And all the air a solemn stillness holds,
Save where the beetle wheels his droning flight,
  And drowsy tinklings lull the distant folds;

Save that from yonder ivy-mantled tower
  The moping owl does to the moon complain
Of such as, wandering near her secret bower,
  Molest her ancient solitary reign.

Beneath those rugged elms, that yew-tree's shade,
  Where heaves the turf in many a mouldering heap,
Each in his narrow cell for ever laid,
  The rude forefathers of the hamlet sleep.

The breezy call of incense-breathing morn,
  The swallow twittering from the straw-built shed,
The cock's shrill clarion, or the echoing horn,
  No more shall rouse them from their lowly bed.

For them no more the blazing hearth shall burn,
  Or busy housewife ply her evening care:
No children run to lisp their sire's return,
  Or climb his knee the envied kiss to share.

Oft did the harvest to their sickle yield,
　Their furrow oft the stubborn glebe has broke:
How jocund did they drive their team afield!
　How bowed the woods beneath their sturdy stroke!

Let not ambition mock their useful toil,
　Their homely joys, and destiny obscure;
Nor grandeur hear with a disdainful smile
　The short and simple annals of the poor.

The boast of heraldry, the pomp of power,
　And all that beauty, all that wealth e'er gave,
Awaits alike the inevitable hour.
　The paths of glory lead but to the grave.

Nor you, ye proud, impute to these the fault,
　If memory o'er their tomb no trophies raise,
Where through the long-drawn aisle and fretted vault
　The pealing anthem swells the note of praise.

Can storied urn or animated bust
　Back to its mansion call the fleeting breath?
Can honour's voice provoke the silent dust,
　Or flattery soothe the dull cold ear of death?

Perhaps in this neglected spot is laid
　Some heart once pregnant with celestial fire;
Hands, that the rod of empire might have swayed,
　Or waked to extasy the living lyre.

But knowledge to their eyes her ample page
　Rich with the spoils of time did ne'er unroll;
Chill penury repressed their noble rage,
　And froze the genial current of the soul.

Full many a gem of purest ray serene,
  The dark unfathomed caves of ocean bear;
Full many a flower is born to blush unseen,
  And waste its sweetness on the desert air.

Some village-Hampden, that with dauntless breast
  The little tyrant of his fields withstood,
Some mute inglorious Milton here may rest,
  Some Cromwell guiltless of his country's blood.

The applause of listening senates to command.
  The threats of pain and ruin to despise,
To scatter plenty o'er a smiling land,
  And read their history in a nation's eyes,

Their lot forbad: nor circumscribed alone
  Their growing virtues, but their crimes confined;
Forbad to wade through slaughter to a throne,
  And shut the gates of mercy on mankind,

The struggling pangs of conscious truth to hide,
  To quench the blushes of ingenuous shame,
Or heap the shrine of luxury and pride
  With incense kindled at the Muse's flame.

Far from the madding crowd's ignoble strife,
  Their sober wishes never learned to stray;
Along the cool sequestered vale of life
  They kept the noiseless tenor of their way.

Yet even these bones from insult to protect
  Some frail memorial still erected nigh,
With uncouth rhymes and shapeless sculpture decked,
  Implores the passing tribute of a sigh.

Their name, their years, spelt by the unlettered Muse,
  The place of fame and elegy supply:
And many a holy text around she strews,
  That teach the rustic moralist to die.

For who, to dumb forgetfulness a prey,
  This pleasing anxious being e'er resigned,
Left the warm precincts of the cheerful day,
  Nor cast one longing lingering look behind?

On some fond breast the parting soul relies,
  Some pious drops the closing eye requires;
E'en from the tomb the voice of nature cries,
  E'en in our ashes live their wonted fires.

For thee, who mindful of the unhonoured dead,
  Dost in these lines their artless tale relate;
If chance, by lonely contemplation led,
  Some kindred spirit shall inquire thy fate –

Haply some hoary-headed swain may say,
  'Oft have we seen him at the peep of dawn
Brushing with hasty steps the dews away
  To meet the sun upon the upland lawn.

'There at the foot of yonder nodding beech,
  That wreathes its old fantastic roots so high,
His listless length at noontide would he stretch,
  And pore upon the brook that babbles by.

'Hard by yon wood, now smiling as in scorn,
  Muttering his wayward fancies he would rove,
Now drooping, woeful-wan, like one forlorn,
  Or crazed with care, or crossed in hopeless love.

'One morn I missed him on the customed hill,
    Along the heath, and near his favourite tree;
Another came; nor yet beside the rill,
    Nor up the lawn, nor at the wood was he:

'The next, with dirges due in sad array
    Slow through the church-way path we saw him
        borne.
Approach and read (for thou can'st read) the lay,
    Graved on the stone beneath yon aged thorn.'

(There scattered oft, the earliest of the year,
    By hands unseen, are showers of violets found:
The redbreast loves to bill and warble there,
    And little footsteps lightly print the ground.)

The Epitaph

Here rests his head upon the lap of Earth
    A Youth, to Fortune and to Fame unknown.
Fair Science frowned not on his humble birth,
    And melancholy marked him for her own.

Large was his bounty, and his soul sincere,
    Heaven did a recompense as largely send:
He gave to Misery all he had, a tear,
    He gained from Heaven ('twas all he wished) a friend.

No farther seek his merits to disclose,
    Or draw his frailties from their dread abode,
(There they alike in trembling hope repose,)
    The bosom of his Father and his God.

The Darkling Thrush

THOMAS HARDY

I leant upon a coppice gate
   When Frost was spectre-gray,
And Winter's dregs made desolate
   The weakening eye of day.
The tangled bine-stems scored the sky
   Like strings of broken lyres,
And all mankind that haunted nigh
   Had sought their household fires.

The land's sharp features seemed to be
   The Century's corpse outleant,
His crypt the cloudy canopy,
   The wind his death-lament.
The ancient pulse of germ and birth
   Was shrunken hard and dry,
And every spirit upon earth
   Seemed fervourless as I.

At once a voice arose among
   The bleak twigs overhead
In a full-hearted evensong
   Of joy illimited;
An aged thrush, frail, gaunt, and small,
   In blast-beruffled plume,
Had chosen thus to fling his soul
   Upon the growing gloom.

So little cause for carolings
   Of such ecstatic sound

Was written on terrestrial things
    Afar or nigh around,
That I could think there trembled through
    His happy good-night air
Some blessed Hope, whereof he knew
    And I was unaware.

The Gate Of The Year

M. LOUISE HASKINS

And I said to the man who stood at the gate of the
  year:
'Give me a light, that I may tread safely into the
  unknown!'
And he replied:
'Go out into the darkness and put your hand into the
  Hand of God.
That shall be to you better than light and safer than a
  known way.'

So, I went forth, and finding the Hand of God, trod
  gladly into the night
And He led me toward the hills and the breaking of
  day in the lone East.

So, heart, be still!
What need our little life,
Our human life, to know,
If God hath comprehension?
In all the dizzy strife
Of things both high and low
God hideth His intention.

Invictus

WILLIAM ERNEST HENLEY

Out of the night that covers me
  Black as the pit from pole to pole,
I thank whatever gods may be
  For my unconquerable soul.

In the fell clutch of circumstance
  I have not winced nor cried aloud.
Under the bludgeonings of chance
  My head is bloody, but unbowed.

Beyond this place of wrath and tears
  Looms but the Horror of the shade,
And yet the menace of the years
  Finds and shall find me unafraid.

It matters not how strait the gate,
  How charged with punishments the scroll,
I am the master of my fate:
  I am the captain of my soul.

The Pulley

GEORGE HERBERT

When God at first made man,
Having a glass of blessings standing by;
Let us (said he) pour on him all we can;
Let the world's riches, which dispersed lie,
    Contract into a span.

So strength first made a way;
Then beauty flowed, then wisdom, honour, pleasure;
When almost all was out, God made a stay,
Perceiving that alone of all his treasure,
    Rest in the bottom lay.

For if I should (said he)
Bestow this jewel also on my creature,
He would adore my gifts instead of me,
And rest in nature, not the God of nature:
    So both should losers be.

Yet let him keep the rest,
But keep them with repining restlessness:
Let him be rich and weary, that at least,
If goodness lead him not, yet weariness
    May toss him to my breast.

The Song Of The Shirt

THOMAS HOOD

With fingers weary and worn,
  With eyelids heavy and red,
A Woman sat, in unwomanly rags,
  Plying her needle and thread –
    Stitch! stitch! stitch!
A little weeping would ease my heart,
  But in their briny bed
My tears must stop, for every drop
    Hinders needle and thread!

Seam, and gusset, and band,
Band, and gusset, and seam,
    Work, work, work,
Like the Engine that works by Steam!
A mere machine of iron and wood
    That toils for Mammon's sake –
Without a brain to ponder and craze
    Or a heart to feel – and break!

With fingers weary and worn,
  With eyelids heavy and red,
A Woman sat in unwomanly rags,
  Plying her needle and thread, –
    Stitch! stitch! stitch!
  In poverty, hunger, and dirt,
And still with a voice of dolorous pitch,
Would that its tone could reach the Rich! –
  She sang this 'Song of the Shirt'!

Duty

ELLEN S. HOOPER

I slept and dreamed that life was Beauty:
I woke and found that life was Duty:
Was then the dream a shadowy lie?
Toil on, sad heart, courageously,
And thou shalt find thy dream to be
A noonday light and truth to thee.

God's Grandeur

GERARD MANLEY HOPKINS

The world is charged with the grandeur of God.
　It will flame out, like shining from shook foil;
　It gathers to a greatness, like the ooze of oil
Crushed. Why do men then now not reck his rod?
Generations have trod, have trod, have trod;
　And all is seared with trade; bleared, smeared with
　　toil;
　And wears man's smudge and shares man's smell: the
　　soil
Is bare now, nor can foot feel, being shod.

And for all this, nature is never spent;
　There lives the dearest freshness deep down things;
And though the last lights off the black West went
　Oh, morning, at the brown brink eastward, springs –
Because the Holy Ghost over the bent
　World broods with warm breast and with ah! bright
　　wings.

Loveliest Of Trees, The Cherry Now

A. E. HOUSMAN

Loveliest of trees, the cherry now
Is hung with bloom along the bough,
And stands about the woodland ride
Wearing white for Eastertide.

Now, of my threescore years and ten,
Twenty will not come again,
And take from seventy springs a score,
It only leaves me fifty more.

And since to look at things in bloom
Fifty springs are little room,
About the woodlands I will go
To see the cherry hung with snow.

Abou Ben Adhem

LEIGH HUNT

Abou Ben Adhem (may his tribe increase!)
Awoke one night from a deep dream of peace,
And saw, within the moonlight in his room,
Making it rich, and like a lily in bloom,
An angel writing in a book of gold:
Exceeding peace had made Ben Adhem bold,
And to the presence in the room he said,
'What writest thou?' The vision raised its head,
And with a look made of all sweet accord,
Answered, 'The names of those who love the Lord.'
'And is mine one?' said Abou. 'Nay, not so,'
Replied the angel. Abou spoke more low,
But cheerly still; and said, 'I pray thee, then,
Write me as one that loves his fellow men.'
The angel wrote, and vanished. The next night
It came again with a great wakening light,
And showed the names whom love of God had blest,
And lo! Ben Adhem's name led all the rest.

Let Me Not See Old Age

D. R. GERAINT JONES

Let me not see old age: Let me not hear
The proffered help, the mumbled sympathy,
The well-meant tactful sophistries that mock
Pathetic husks who once were strong and free,
And in youth's fickle triumph laughed and sang,
Loved, and were foolish; and at the close have seen
The fruits of folly garnered, and that love,
Tamed and encaged, stale into grey routine.
Let me not see old age; I am content
With my few crowded years; laughter and strength
And song have lit the beacon of my life.
Let me not see it fade, but when the long
September shadows steal across the square,
Grant me this wish; they may not find me there.

Warning

JENNY JOSEPH

When I am an old woman I shall wear purple
With a red hat which doesn't go, and doesn't suit me,
And I shall spend my pension on brandy and summer
  gloves
And satin sandals, and say we've no money for butter.
I shall sit down on the pavement when I'm tired
And gobble up samples in shops and press alarm bells
And run my stick along the public railings
And make up for the sobriety of my youth.
I shall go out in my slippers in the rain
And pick the flowers in other people's gardens
And learn to spit.

You can wear terrible shirts and grow more fat
And eat three pounds of sausages at a go
Or only bread and pickle for a week
And hoard pens and pencils and beermats and things in
  boxes.

But now we must have clothes that keep us dry
And pay our rent and not swear in the street
And set a good example for the children.
We will have friends to dinner and read the papers.

But maybe I ought to practise a little now?
So people who know me are not too shocked and
  surprised
When suddenly I am old and start to wear purple.

Meg Merrilies

JOHN KEATS

Old Meg she was a gipsy,
  And lived upon the moors;
Her bed it was the brown heath turf,
  And her house was out of doors.

Her apples were swart blackberries,
  Her currants, pods o' broom;
Her wine was dew of the wild white rose,
  Her book a churchyard tomb.

Her brothers were the craggy hills,
  Her sisters larchen trees;
Alone with her great family
  She lived as she did please.

No breakfast had she many a morn,
  No dinner many a noon,
And 'stead of supper she would stare
  Full hard against the moon.

But every morn, of woodbine fresh
  She made her garlanding,
And every night the dark glen yew
  She wove, and she would sing.

And with her fingers, old and brown,
  She plaited mats o' rushes,
And gave them to the cottagers
  She met among the bushes.

Old Meg was brave as Margaret Queen
  And tall as Amazon;
An old red blanket cloak she wore,
  A chip hat had she on.
God rest her aged bones somewhere;
  She died full long agone!

Ode To The North-East Wind

CHARLES KINGSLEY

Welcome, wild North-easter.
  Shame it is to see
Odes to every zephyr;
  Ne'er a verse to thee.
Welcome, black North-easter!
  O'er the German foam;
O'er the Danish moorlands,
  From thy frozen home.
Tired we are of summer,
  Tired of gaudy glare,
Showers soft and steaming,
  Hot and breathless air.
Tired of listless dreaming,
  Through the lazy day:
Jovial wind of winter,
  Turn us out to play!
Sweep the golden reed-beds;
  Crisp the lazy dyke;
Hunger into madness
  Every plunging pike.
Fill the lake with wild-fowl;
  Fill the marsh with snipe;
While on dreary moorlands
  Lonely curlew pipe.

Through the black fir-forest
  Thunder harsh and dry,
Shattering down the snow-flakes
  Off the curdled sky.

Hark! The brave North-easter!
  Breast-high lies the scent,
On by holt and headland,
  Over heath and bent.
Chime, ye dappled darlings,
  Through the sleet and snow.
Who can over-ride you?
  Let the horses go!
Chime, ye dappled darlings,
  Down the roaring blast;
You shall see a fox die
  Ere an hour be past.
Go! and rest to-morrow,
  Hunting in your dreams,
While our skates are ringing
  O'er the frozen streams.
Let the luscious South-wind
  Breathe in lovers' sighs,
While the lazy gallants
  Bask in ladies' eyes.

What does he but soften
  Heart alike and pen?
'Tis the hard grey weather
  Breeds hard English men.
What's the soft South-wester?
  'Tis the ladies' breeze,
Bringing home their true-loves
  Out of all the seas:
But the black North-easter,
  Through the snowstorm hurled,
Drives our English hearts of oak
  Seaward round the world.
Come, as came our fathers,

Heralded by thee,
Conquering from the eastward,
  Lords by land and sea.
Come; and strong within us
  Stir the Viking's blood;
Bracing brain and sinew;
  Blow, thou wind of God!

The Glory Of The Garden

RUDYARD KIPLING

Our England is a garden that is full of stately views,
Of borders, beds and shrubberies and lawns and
  avenues,
With statues on the terraces and peacocks strutting by;
But the Glory of the Garden lies in more than meets
  the eye.

For where the old thick laurels grow, along the thin
  red wall,
You find the tool- and potting-sheds which are the
  heart of all;
The cold-frames and the hot-houses, the dungpits and
  the tanks,
The rollers, carts and drain-pipes, with the barrows and
  the planks.

And there you'll see the gardeners, the men and
  'prentice boys
Told off to do as they are bid and do it without noise;
For, except when seeds are planted and we shout to
  scare the birds,
The Glory of the Garden it abideth not in words.

And some can pot begonias and some can bud a rose,
And some are hardly fit to trust with anything that
  grows;
But they can roll and trim the lawns and sift the sand
  and loam,
For the Glory of the Garden occupieth all who come.

Our England is a garden, and such gardens are not
  made
By singing:– 'Oh, how beautiful!' and sitting in the
  shade,
While better men than we go out and start their
  working lives
At grubbing weeds from gravel-paths with broken
  dinner-knives.

There's not a pair of legs so thin, there's not a head so
  thick,
There's not a hand so weak and white, nor yet a heart
  so sick,
But it can find some needful job that's crying to be
  done,
For the Glory of the Garden glorifieth every one.

Then seek your job with thankfulness and work till
  further orders,
If it's only netting strawberries or killing slugs on
  borders;
And when your back stops aching and your hands
  begin to harden,
You will find yourself a partner in the Glory of the
  Garden.

Oh, Adam was a gardener, and God who made him
  sees
That half a proper gardener's work is done upon his
  knees,
So when your work is finished, you can wash your
  hands and pray
For the Glory of the Garden, that it may not pass
  away!
And the Glory of the Garden it shall never pass away!

Love Songs In Age

PHILIP LARKIN

She kept her songs, they took so little space,
   The covers pleased her:
One bleached from lying in a sunny place,
One marked in circles by a vase of water,
One mended, when a tidy fit had seized her,
   And coloured, by her daughter –
So they had waited, till in widowhood
She found them, looking for something else, and stood

Relearning how each frank submissive chord
   Had ushered in
Word after sprawling hyphenated word,
And the unfailing sense of being young
Spread out like a spring-woken tree, wherein
   That hidden freshness sung,
That certainty of time laid up in store
As when she played them first. But, even more,

The glare of that much-mentioned brilliance, love,
   Broke out, to show
Its bright incipience sailing above,
Still promising to solve, and satisfy,
And set unchangeably in order. So
   To pile them back, to cry
Was hard, without lamely admitting how
It had not done so then, and could not now.

Snake

D. H. LAWRENCE

A snake came to my water-trough
On a hot, hot day, and I in pyjamas for the heat,
To drink there.

In the deep, strange-scented shade of the great dark
  carob-tree
I came down the steps with my pitcher
And must wait, must stand and wait, for there he was
  at the trough before me.

He reached down from a fissure in the earth-wall in
  the gloom
And trailed his yellow-brown slackness soft-bellied
  down, over the edge of the stone trough
And rested his throat upon the stone bottom,
And where the water had dripped from the tap, in a
  small clearness,
He sipped with his straight mouth,
Softly drank through his straight gums, into his slack
  long body,
Silently.

Someone was before me at my water-trough,
And I, like a second comer, waiting.

He lifted his head from his drinking, as cattle do,
And looked at me vaguely, as drinking cattle do,
And flickered his two-forked tongue from his lips, and
  mused a moment,

And stooped and drank a little more,
Being earth-brown, earth-golden from the burning
  bowels of the earth
On the day of Sicilian July, with Etna smoking.

The voice of my education said to me
He must be killed,
For in Sicily the black, black snakes are innocent, the
  gold are venomous.

And voices in me said, If you were a man
You would take a stick and break him now, and finish
  him off.

But must I confess how I liked him,
How glad I was he had come like a guest in quiet, to
  drink at my water-trough
And depart peaceful, pacified, and thankless,
Into the burning bowels of this earth?

Was it cowardice, that I dared not kill him?
Was it perversity, that I longed to talk to him?
Was it humility, to feel so honoured?
I felt so honoured.

And yet those voices:
If you were not afraid, you would kill him!

And truly I was afraid, I was most afraid,
But even so, honoured still more
That he should seek my hospitality
From out the dark door of the secret earth.

He drank enough
And lifted his head, dreamily, as one who has drunken,
And flickered his tongue like a forked night on the air,
  so black,
Seeming to lick his lips,
And looked around like a god, unseeing, into the air,
And slowly turned his head,
And slowly, very slowly, as if thrice adream,
Proceeded to draw his slow length curving round
And climb again the broken bank of my wall-face.

And as he put his head into that dreadful hole,
And as he slowly drew up, snake-easing his shoulders,
  and entered farther,
A sort of horror, a sort of protest against his
  withdrawing into that horrid black hole,
Deliberately going into the blackness, and slowly
  drawing himself after,
Overcame me now his back was turned.

I looked round, I put down my pitcher,
I picked up a clumsy log
And threw it at the water-trough with a clatter.

I think it did not hit him,
But suddenly that part of him that was left behind
  convulsed in undignified haste,
Writhed like lightning, and was gone
Into the black hole, the earth-lipped fissure in the wall-
  front,
At which, in the intense still noon, I stared with
  fascination.

And immediately I regretted it.
I thought how paltry, how vulgar, what a mean act!
I despised myself and the voices of my accursed human
  education.
And I thought of the albatross,
And I wished he would come back, my snake.

For he seemed to me again like a king,
Like a king in exile, uncrowned in the underworld,
Now due to be crowned again.

And so, I missed my chance with one of the lords
Of life.
And I have something to expiate;
A pettiness.

A Wish

LAURENCE LERNER

Often I've wished that I'd been born a woman.
It seems the one sure way to be fully human.
Think of the trouble – keeping the children fed,
Keeping your skirt down and your lips red,
Watching the calendar and the last bus home,
Being nice to all the dozens of guests in the room;
Having to change your hairstyle and your name
At least once; learning to take the blame;
Keeping your husband faithful, and your char.
And all the things you're supposed to be grateful for
– Votes and proposals, chocolates and seats in the
   train –
Or expert with – typewriter, powderpuff, pen,
Diaphragm, needle, chequebook, casserole, bed.
It seems the one sure way to be driven mad.

So why would anyone want to be a woman?
Would you rather be the hero or the victim?
Would you rather win, seduce, and read the paper,
Or be beaten, pregnant, and have to lay the table?
Nothing is free. In order to pay the price
Isn't it simpler, really, to have no choice?
Only ill-health, recurring, inevitable,
Can teach the taste of what it is to be well.

No man has ever felt his daughter tear
The flesh he had earlier torn to plant her there.
Men know the pain of birth by a kind of theory:
No man has been a protagonist in the story,

Lying back bleeding, exhausted and in pain,
Waiting for stitches and sleep and to be alone,
And listened with tender breasts to the hesitant croak
At the bedside growing continuous as you wake.
That is the price. That is what love is worth.
It will go on twisting your heart like an afterbirth.
Whether you choose to or not you will pay and pay
Your whole life long. Nothing on earth is free.

Walking Away

C. DAY LEWIS

It is eighteen years ago, almost to the day –
A sunny day with the leaves just turning,
The touch-lines new-ruled – since I watched you play
Your first game of football, then, like a satellite
Wrenched from its orbit, go drifting away

Behind a scatter of boys. I can see
You walking away from me towards the school
With the pathos of a half-fledged thing set free
Into a wilderness, the gait of one
Who finds no path where the path should be.

That hesitant figure, eddying away
Like a winged seed loosened from its parent stem,
Has something I never quite grasp to convey
About nature's give-and-take – the small, the scorching
Ordeals which fire one's irresolute clay.

I have had worse partings, but none that so
Gnaws at my mind still. Perhaps it is roughly
Saying what God alone could perfectly show –
How selfhood begins with a walking away,
And love is proved in the letting go.

The Legend Beautiful from 'The Theologian's Tale'

HENRY WADSWORTH LONGFELLOW

'Hadst thou stayed, I must have fled!'
That is what the Vision said.

In his chamber all alone,
Kneeling on the floor of stone,
Prayed the Monk in deep contrition
For his sins of indecision,
Prayed for greater self-denial
In temptation and in trial;
It was noonday by the dial,
And the Monk was all alone.

Suddenly, as if it lightened,
An unwonted splendour brightened
All within him and without him
In that narrow cell of stone;
And he saw the Blessed Vision
Of our Lord, with light Elysian
Like a vesture wrapped about him,
Like a garment round him thrown.
Not as crucified and slain,
Not in agonies of pain,
Not with bleeding hands and feet,
Did the Monk his Master see;
But as in the village street,
In the house or harvest-field,
Halt and lame and blind he healed,
When he walked in Galilee.

In an attitude imploring,
Hands upon his bosom crossed,
Wondering, worshipping, adoring,
Knelt the Monk in rapture lost.
Lord, he thought, in heaven that reignest,
Who am I, that thus thou deignest
To reveal thyself to me?
Who am I, that from the centre
Of thy glory thou shouldst enter
This poor cell, my guest to be?

Then amid his exaltation,
Loud the convent bell appalling,
From its belfry calling, calling,
Rang through court and corridor
With persistent iteration
He had never heard before.
It was now the appointed hour
When alike in shine or shower,
Winter's cold or summer's heat,
To the convent portals came
All the blind and halt and lame,
All the beggars of the street,
For their daily dole of food
Dealt them by the brotherhood;
And their almoner was he
Who upon his bended knee,
Rapt in silent ecstasy
Of divinest self-surrender,
Saw the Vision and the Splendour.

Deep distress and hesitation
Mingled with his adoration;
Should he go, or should he stay?

Should he leave the poor to wait
Hungry at the convent gate,
Till the Vision passed away?
Should he slight his radiant guest,
Slight this visitant celestial,
For the crowd of ragged, bestial
Beggars at the convent gate?
Would the Vision there remain?
Would the Vision come again?
Then a voice within his breast
Whispered, audible and clear
As if to the outward ear:
'Do thy duty; that is best;
Leave unto thy Lord the rest!'

Straightway to his feet he started,
And with longing look intent
On the Blessed Vision bent,
Slowly from his cell departed,
Slowly on his errand went.
At the gate the poor were waiting,
Looking through the iron grating,
With that terror in the eye
That is only seen in those
Who amid their wants and woes
Hear the sound of doors that close,
And of feet that pass them by;
Grown familiar with disfavour,
Grown familiar with the savour
Of the bread by which men die!
But today, they knew not why,
Like the gate of Paradise
Seemed the convent gate to rise,
Like a sacrament divine,

Seemed to them the bread and wine.
In his heart the Monk was praying,
Thinking of the homeless poor,
What they suffer and endure;
What we see not, what we see;
And the inward voice was saying:
'Whatsoever thing thou doest
To the least of mine and lowest,
That thou doest unto me!'

Unto me! but had the Vision
Come to him in beggar's clothing,
Come a mendicant imploring,
Would he then have knelt adoring,
Or have listened with derision,
And have turned away with loathing?

Thus his conscience put the question,
Full of troublesome suggestion,
As at length, with hurried pace,
Towards his cell he turned his face,
And beheld the convent bright,
With a supernatural light,
Like a luminous cloud expanding
Over floor and wall and ceiling.
But he paused with awe-struck feeling
At the threshold of his door,
For the Vision still was standing
As he left it there before,
When the convent bell appalling,
From its belfry calling, calling,
Summoned him to feed the poor.
Through the long hour intervening
It had waited his return,

And he felt his bosom burn,
Comprehending all the meaning,
When the Blessed Vision said,
'Hadst thou stayed, I must have fled!'

Oxford

TOM LOVATT-WILLIAMS

I see the coloured lilacs flame
In many an ancient Oxford lane
And bright laburnum holds its bloom
Suspended golden in the noon,
The placid lawns I often tread
Are stained and carpeted with red
Where the tall chestnuts cast their flowers
To mark the fleeting April hours,
And now the crowded hawthorn yields
Its haunting perfume to the fields
With men and maidens hurrying out
Along Port Meadow to the Trout,
There, by the coruscating stream
To drink and gaze and gaze and dream;
An ageless dame leaves her abode
To caper down the Woodstock Road
And greet a Dean she used to know
A trifling sixty years ago.
Queer tricycles of unknown date
Are pedalled at a frightful rate
Their baskets bulge with borrowed books
Or terriers of uncertain looks.

Perpetual motion in The High
Beneath a blue and primrose sky
And cherry blossom like a cloud
Beside the traffic roaring loud,
While daffodils go dancing gold
In streets where time runs grey and old

And poets, sweating in the throng,
Can sometimes hear a blackbird's song.
All Oxford's spires are tipped with rose
A wind full magic sweetly blows
And suddenly it seems in truth
As if the centuries of youth
Are crowding all the streets and lanes
In April when the lilac flames.

So What Is Love?

MARIA LOVELL (trans.)

So what is love? If thou wouldst know
The heart alone can tell:
Two minds with but a single thought,
Two hearts that beat as one.

And whence comes Love? Like morning bright
Love comes without thy call.
And how dies Love? A spirit bright,
Love never dies at all.

Prayer Before Birth

LOUIS MACNEICE

I am not yet born; O hear me.
Let not the bloodsucking bat or the rat or the stoat or the
    club-footed ghoul come near me.

I am not yet born, console me.
I fear that the human race may with tall walls wall me,
    with strong drugs dope me, with wise lies lure me,
      on black racks rack me, in blood-baths roll me.

I am not yet born; provide me
With water to dandle me, grass to grow for me, trees to talk
    to me, sky to sing to me, birds and a white light
      in the back of my mind to guide me.

I am not yet born; forgive me
For the sins that in me the world shall commit, my
    words when they speak me, my thoughts when they
      think me, my treason engendered by traitors
        beyond me, my life when they murder by means
          of my hands, my death when they live me.

I am not yet born; rehearse me
In the parts I must play and the cues I must take when
    old men lecture me, bureaucrats hector me, mountains
      frown at me, lovers laugh at me, the white
        waves call me to folly and the desert calls
          me to doom and the beggar refuses
            my gift and my children curse me.

I am not yet born; O hear me,
Let not the man who is beast or who thinks he is God
   come near me.

I am not yet born; O fill me
With strength against those who would freeze my
   humanity, would dragoon me into a lethal automaton,
     would make me a cog in a machine, a thing with
      one face, a thing, and against all those
       who would dissipate my entirety, would
        blow me like thistledown hither and
         thither or hither and thither
          like water held in the
           hands would spill me.

Let them not make me a stone and let them not spill me.
Otherwise kill me.

High Flight (An Airman's Ecstasy)

JOHN GILLESPIE MAGEE

Oh, I have slipped the surly bonds of earth
And danced the skies on laughter-silvered wings;
Sunward I've climbed and joined the tumbling mirth
Of sun-split clouds – and done a hundred things
You have not dreamed of; wheeled and soared and swung
High in the sun-lit silence. Hovering there
I've chased the shouting wind along, and flung
My eager craft through footless halls of air;
Up, up the long, delirious, burning blue
I've topped the wind-swept heights with easy grace,
Where never lark nor even eagle flew;
And while, with silent lifting mind I've trod
The high untrespassed sanctity of space,
Put out my hand, and touched the face of God.

Nicholas Nye

WALTER DE LA MARE

Thistle and darnel and dock grew there,
  And a bush, in the corner, of may,
On the orchard wall I used to sprawl
  In the blazing heat of the day;
Half asleep and half awake,
  While the birds went twittering by,
And nobody there my lone to share
    But Nicholas Nye.

Nicholas Nye was lean and grey,
  Lame of a leg and old,
More than a score of donkey's years
  He had seen since he was foaled;
He munched the thistles, purple and spiked,
  Would sometimes stoop and sigh,
And turn his head, as if he said,
    'Poor Nicholas Nye!'

Alone with his shadow he'd drowse in the meadow,
  Lazily swinging his tail,
At break of day he used to bray, –
  Not much too hearty and hale;
But a wonderful gumption was under his skin,
  And a clear calm light in his eye,
And once in a while he'd smile . . .
    Would Nicholas Nye.

Seem to be smiling at me, he would,
  From his bush in the corner, of may, –

Bony and ownerless, widowed and worn,
  Knobble-kneed, lonely and grey;
And over the grass would seem to pass
  'Neath the deep dark blue of the sky,
Something much better than words between me
  And Nicholas Nye.

But dusk would come in the apple boughs,
  The green of the glow-worm shine,
The birds in the nest would crouch to rest,
  And home I'd trudge to mine;
And there, in the moonlight, dark with dew,
  Asking not wherefore nor why,
Would brood like a ghost, and still as a post.
  Old Nicholas Nye.

The Life That I Have

LEO MARKS

The life that I have
Is all that I have
And the life that I have
Is yours

The love that I have
Of the life that I have
Is yours and yours and yours

A sleep I shall have
A rest I shall have
Yet death will be but a pause

For the peace of my years
In the long green grass
Will be yours and yours and yours

Sea-Fever

JOHN MASEFIELD

I must down to the seas again, to the lonely sea and
the sky,
And all I ask is a tall ship and a star to steer her by,
And the wheel's kick and the wind's song and the
white sail's shaking,
And a grey mist on the sea's face and a grey dawn
breaking.

I must down to the seas again, for the call of the
running tide
Is a wild call and a clear call that may not be denied;
And all I ask is a windy day with the white clouds
flying,
And the flung spray and the blown spume, and the
sea-gulls crying.

I must down to the seas again, to the vagrant gypsy
life,
To the gull's way and the whale's way where the
wind's like a whetted knife;
And all I ask is a merry yarn from a laughing fellow-
rover,
And quiet sleep and a sweet dream when the long
trick's over.

The Farmer's Bride

CHARLOTTE MEW

Three Summers since I chose a maid,
Too young maybe – but more's to do
At harvest-time than bide and woo.
   When us was wed she turned afraid
Of love and me and all things human;
Like the shut of a winter's day
Her smile went out, and 'twadn't a woman –
   More like a little frightened fay.
   One night, in the Fall, she runned away.

'Out 'mong the sheep, her be,' they said,
'Should properly have been abed';
But sure enough she wadn't there
Lying awake with her wide brown stare.
So over seven-acre field and up-along across the down
We chased her, flying like a hare
Before our lanterns. To Church-Town
   All in a shiver and a scare
We caught her, fetched her home at last
   And turned the key upon her, fast.

She does the work about the house
As well as must, but like a mouse:
   Happy enough to chat and play
   With birds and rabbits and such as they,
   So long as men-folk keep away.
'Not near, not near!' her eyes beseech
When one of us comes within reach.
   The women say that beasts in stall

Look round like children at her call.
I've hardly heard her speak at all.

Shy as a leveret, swift as he,
Straight and slight as a young larch tree,
Sweet as the first wild violets, she,
To her wild self. But what to me?

The short days shorten and the oaks are brown,
   The blue smoke rises to the low grey sky,
One leaf in the still air falls slowly down,
   A magpie's spotted feathers lie
On the black earth spread white with rime,
The berries redden up to Christmas-time.
   What's Christmas-time without there be
   Some other in the house than we!

   She sleeps up in the attic there
   Alone, poor maid. 'Tis but a stair
Betwixt us. Oh! my God! the down,
   The soft young down of her, the brown,
The brown of her – her eyes, her hair, her hair!

Renouncement

ALICE MEYNELL

I must not think of thee; and, tired yet strong,
I shun the love that lurks in all delight –
  The love of thee – and in the blue heaven's height,
And in the dearest passage of a song.
Oh, just beyond the sweetest thoughts that throng
  This breast, the thought of thee waits hidden yet
    bright;
But it must never, never come in sight;
I must stop short of thee the whole day long.
But when sleep comes to close each difficult day,
  When night gives pause to the long watch I keep,
And all my bonds I needs must loose apart,
Must doff my will as raiment laid away, –
  With the first dream that comes with the first sleep
I run, I run, I am gathered to thy heart.

Dirge Without Music

EDNA ST VINCENT MILLAY

I am not resigned to the shutting away of loving hearts
  in the hard ground
So it is, and so it will be, for so it has been, time out
  of mind:
Into the darkness they go, the wise and the lovely.
  Crowned
With lilies and with laurel they go: but I am not
  resigned.

Lovers and thinkers, into the earth with you.
Be one with the dull, the indiscriminate dust.
A fragment of what you felt, of what you knew,
A formula, a phrase remains – but the best is lost.

The answers quick and keen, the honest look, the
  laughter, the love –
They are gone. They have gone to feed the roses.
  Elegant and curled
Is the blossom. Fragrant is the blossom. I know. But I
  do not approve.
More precious was the light in your eyes than all the
  roses in the world.

Down, down, down into the darkness of the grave
Gently they go, the beautiful, the tender, the kind:
Quietly they go, the intelligent, the witty, the brave.
I know. But I do not approve. And I am not resigned.

Dunkirk (A Ballad)

ROBERT NATHAN

Will came back from school that day,
And he had little to say.
But he stood a long time looking down
To where the gray-green Channel water
Slapped at the foot of the little town,
And to where his boat, the Sarah P,
Bobbed at the tide on an even keel
With her one old sail, patched at the leech,
Furled like a slattern down at heel.

He stood for a while above the beach,
He saw how the wind and current caught her;
He looked a long time out to sea.
There was steady wind, and the sky was pale,
And a haze in the east that looked like smoke.

Will went back to the house to dress.
He was half way through, when his sister Bess
Who was near fourteen, and younger than he
By just two years, came home from play.
She asked him, 'Where are you going, Will?'
He said, 'For a good long sail.'
'Can I come along?'
                    'No, Bess,' he spoke.
'I may be gone for a night and a day.'
Bess looked at him. She kept very still.
She had heard the news of the Flanders rout,
How the English were trapped above Dunkirk,
And the fleet had gone to get them out —

But everyone thought that it wouldn't work.
There was too much fear, there was too much doubt.

She looked at him, and he looked at her.
They were English children, born and bred.
He frowned her down, but she wouldn't stir.
She shook her proud young head.
'You'll need a crew,' she said.

They raised the sail on the Sarah P,
Like a penoncel on a young knight's lance,
And headed the Sarah out to sea,
To bring their soldiers home from France.

There was no command, there was no set plan,
But six hundred boats went out with them
On the gray-green waters, sailing fast,
River excursion and fisherman,
Tug and schooner and racing M,
And the little boats came following last.
From every harbor and town they went
Who had sailed their craft in the sun and rain,
From the South Downs, from the cliffs of Kent,
From the village street, from the country lane.

There are twenty miles of rolling sea
From coast to coast, by the seagull's flight,
But the tides were fair and the wind was free,
And they raised Dunkirk by fall of night.

They raised Dunkirk with its harbor torn
By the blasted stern and the sunken prow;
They had raced for fun on an English tide,
They were English children bred and born,

And whether they lived, or whether they died,
They raced for England now.

Bess was as white as the Sarah's sail,
She set her teeth and smiled at Will.
He held his course for the smoky veil
Where the harbor narrowed thin and long.
The British ships were firing strong.

He took the Sarah into his hands,
He drove her in through fire and death
To the wet men waiting on the sands.
He got his load and he got his breath,
And she came about, and the wind fought her.

He shut his eyes and he tried to pray.
He saw his England where she lay,
The wind's green home, the sea's proud daughter,
Still in the moonlight, dreaming deep,
The English cliffs and the English loam –
He had fourteen men to get away,
And the moon was clear, and the night like day
For planes to see where the white sails creep
Over the black water.

He closed his eyes and he prayed for her;
He prayed to the men who had made her great,
Who had built her land of forest and park,
Who had made the seas an English lake;
He prayed for a fog to bring the dark;
He prayed to get home for England's sake.
And the fog came down on the rolling sea,
And covered the ships with English mist.
The diving planes were baffled and blind.

For Nelson was there in the Victory,
With his one good eye, and his sullen twist,
And guns were out on The Golden Hind,
Their shot flashed over the Sarah P.
He could hear them cheer as he came about.

By burning wharves, by battered slips,
Galleon, frigate, and brigantine,
The old dead Captains fought their ships,
And the great dead Admirals led the line.
It was England's night, it was England's sea.

The fog rolled over the harbor key.
Bess held to the stays, and conned him out.
And all through the dark, while the Sarah's wake
Hissed behind him, and vanished in foam,
There at his side sat Francis Drake,
And held him true, and steered him home.

The Highwayman

ALFRED NOYES

I

The wind was a torrent of darkness among the gusty
   trees,
The moon was a ghostly galleon tossed upon cloudy
   seas,
The road was a ribbon of moonlight over the purple
   moor,
And the highwayman came riding –
         Riding – riding –
The highwayman came riding, up to the old inn-door.

He'd a French cocked-hat on his forehead, a bunch of
   lace at his chin,
A coat of claret velvet, and breeches of brown doe-
   skin;
They fitted with never a wrinkle: his boots were up to
   the thigh!
And he rode with a jewelled twinkle,
         His pistol butts a-twinkle,
His rapier hilt a-twinkle, under the jewelled sky.

Over the cobbles he clattered and clashed in the dark
   inn-yard,
And he tapped with his whip on the shutters, but all
   was locked and barred;
He whistled a tune to the window, and who should be
   waiting there
But the landlord's black-eyed daughter,
         Bess, the landlord's daughter,
Plaiting a dark red love-knot into her long black hair.

And dark in the old inn-yard a stable-wicket creaked
Where Tim the ostler listened; his face was white and
  peaked;
His eyes were hollows of madness, his hair like
  mouldy hay,
But he loved the landlord's daughter,
          The landlord's red-lipped daughter;
Dumb as a dog he listened, and he heard the robber
  say —

'One kiss, my bonny sweetheart, I'm after a prize to-
  night,
But I shall be back with the yellow gold before the
  morning light;
Yet, if they press me sharply, and harry me through
  the day,
Then look for me by moonlight,
          Watch for me by moonlight,
I'll come to thee by moonlight, though hell should bar
  the way.'

He rose upright in the stirrups; he scarce could reach
  her hand,
But she loosened her hair i' the casement! His face
  burnt like a brand
As the black cascade of perfume came tumbling over
  his breast;
And he kissed its waves in the moonlight,
          (Oh, sweet black waves in the moonlight!)
Then he tugged at his rein in the moonlight, and
  galloped away to the west.

2

He did not come in the dawning; he did not come at
  noon;
And out o' the tawny sunset, before the rise o' the
  moon,
When the road was a gipsy's ribbon, looping the
  purple moor,
A red-coat troop came marching –
          Marching – marching –
King George's men came marching, up to the old inn-
  door.

They said no word to the landlord, they drank his ale
  instead,
But they gagged his daughter and bound her to the
  foot of her narrow bed;
Two of them knelt at her casement, with muskets at
  their side!
There was death at every window;
          And hell at one dark window;
For Bess could see, through her casement, the road that
  he would ride.
They had tied her up to attention, with many a
  sniggering jest;
They had bound a musket beside her, with the barrel
  beneath her breast!

'Now keep good watch!' and they kissed her.
          She heard the dead man say –
Look for me by moonlight;
          Watch for me by moonlight;
I'll come to thee by moonlight, though hell should bar the way!

She twisted her hands behind her; but all the knots
  held good!

She writhed her hands till her fingers were wet with
  sweat or blood!
They stretched and strained in the darkness, and the
  hours crawled by like years,
Till, now, on the stroke of midnight,
              Cold, on the stroke of midnight,
The tip of one finger touched it! The trigger at least
  was hers!

The tip of one finger touched it; she strove no more
  for the rest!
Up, she stood to attention, with the barrel beneath her
  breast,
She would not risk their hearing; she would not strive
  again;
For the road lay bare in the moonlight;
              Blank and bare in the moonlight;
And the blood of her veins in the moonlight throbbed
  to her love's refrain.

Tlot-tlot; tlot-tlot! Had they heard it? The horse-hoofs
  ringing clear;
Tlot-tlot, tlot-tlot, in the distance? Were they deaf that
  they did not hear?
Down the ribbon of moonlight, over the brow of the
  hill,
The highwayman came riding,
              Riding, riding!
The red-coats looked to their priming! She stood up,
  straight and still!

Tlot-tlot, in the frosty silence! tlot-tlot, in the echoing
  night!

Nearer he came and nearer! Her face was like a light!
Her eyes grew wide for a moment; she drew one last
  deep breath,
Then her finger moved in the moonlight,
            Her musket shattered the moonlight,
Shattered her breast in the moonlight and warned him
  – with her death.
He turned; he spurred to the westward; he did not
  know who stood
Bowed, with her head o'er the musket, drenched with
  her own red blood!
Not till the dawn he heard it, and slowly blanched to
  hear
How Bess, the landlord's daughter,
            The landlord's black-eyed daughter,
Had watched for her love in the moonlight, and died
  in the darkness there.

Back, he spurred like a madman, shrieking a curse to
  the sky,
With the white road smoking behind him and his
  rapier brandished high!
Blood-red were his spurs i' the golden noon; wine-red
  was his velvet coat;
When they shot him down on the highway,
            Down like a dog on the highway,
And he lay in his blood on the highway, with the
  bunch of lace at his throat.

And still of a winter's night, they say, when the wind is in the
  trees,
When the moon is a ghostly galleon tossed upon cloudy seas,
When the road is a ribbon of moonlight over the purple moor,

A highwayman comes riding —
   Riding — riding —
A highwayman comes riding, up to the old inn-door.

Over the cobbles he clatters and clangs in the dark inn-yard
And he taps with his whip on the shutters, but all is locked and
 barred;
He whistles a tune to the window, and who should be waiting there
But the landlord's black-eyed daughter,
   Bess, the landlord's daughter,
Plaiting a dark red love-knot into her long black hair.

Adieu! And Au Revoir

JOHN OXENHAM

As you love me, let there be
No mourning when I go, –
No tearful eyes,
No hopeless sighs,
No woe, – nor even sadness!
Indeed I would not have you sad,
For I myself shall be full glad,
With the high triumphant gladness
Of a soul made free
Of God's sweet liberty.
– No windows darkened;

For my own
Will be flung wide as ne'er before,
To catch the radiant inpour
Of Love that shall in full atone
For all the ills that I have done;
And the good things left undone;
– No voices hushed;
My own, full flushed
With an immortal hope, will rise
In ecstasies of new-born bliss
And joyful melodies.

Rather, of your sweet courtesy,
Rejoice with me
At my soul's loosing from captivity.
Wish me 'Bon Voyage!'
As you do a friend

Whose joyous visit finds its happy end.
And bid me both 'à Dieu!'
And 'au revoir!'
Since, though I come no more,
I shall be waiting there to greet you,
At His Door.

And, as the feet of The Bearers tread
The ways I trod,
Think not of me as dead,
But rather –
'Happy, thrice happy, he whose course is sped!
He has gone home – to God,
His Father!'

The Toys from 'The Unknown Eros'

COVENTRY PATMORE

My little Son, who looked from thoughtful eyes
And moved and spoke in quiet grown-up wise,
Having my law the seventh time disobeyed,
I struck him, and dismissed
With hard words and unkissed,
– His Mother, who was patient, being dead.
Then, fearing lest his grief should hinder sleep,
I visited his bed,
But found him slumbering deep,
With darkened eyelids, and their lashes yet
From his late sobbing wet.
And I, with moan,
Kissing away his tears, left others of my own;
For, on a table drawn beside his head,
He had put, within his reach,
A box of counters and a red-veined stone,
A piece of glass abraded by the beach,
And six or seven shells,
A bottle with bluebells,
And two French copper coins, ranged there with
  careful art,
To comfort his sad heart.

So when that night I prayed
To God, I wept, and said:
'Ah, when at last we lie with trancèd breath,
Not vexing Thee in death,
And Thou rememberest of what toys
We made our joys,

How weakly understood
Thy great commanded good,
Then, fatherly not less
Than I whom Thou hast moulded from the clay,
Thou'lt leave Thy wrath, and say,
"I will be sorry for their childishness." '

from Goblin Market

CHRISTINA ROSSETTI

Morning and evening
Maids heard the goblins cry:
'Come buy our orchard fruits,
Come buy, come buy:
Apples and quinces,
Lemons and oranges,
Plump unpecked cherries,
Melons and raspberries,
Bloom-down-cheeked peaches,
Swart-headed mulberries,
Wild free-born cranberries,
Crab-apples, dewberries,
Pine-apples, blackberries,
Apricots, strawberries; –
All ripe together
In summer weather, –
Morns that pass by,
Fair eves that fly;
Come buy, come buy:
Our grapes fresh from the vine,
Pomegranates full and fine,
Dates and sharp bullaces,
Rare pears and greengages,
Damsons and bilberries,
Taste them and try:
Currants and gooseberries,
Bright-fire-like barberries,
Figs to fill your mouth,
Citrons from the South,

Sweet to tongue and sound to eye;
Come buy, come buy.'

from Canto Sixth (1)
of The Lay Of The Last Minstrel

SIR WALTER SCOTT

Breathes there the man, with soul so dead,
Who never to himself hath said,
  This is my own, my native land!
Whose heart hath ne'er within him burn'd,
As home his footsteps he hath turn'd,
  From wandering on a foreign strand!
If such there breathe, go, mark him well;
For him no Minstrel raptures swell;
High though his titles, proud his name,
Boundless his wealth as wish can claim;
Despite those titles, power, and pelf,
The wretch, concentrated all in self,
Living, shall forfeit fair renown,
And, doubly dying, shall go down
To the vile dust, from whence he sprung,
Unwept, unhonour'd, and unsung.

Shall I Compare Thee To A Summer's Day?

WILLIAM SHAKESPEARE

Shall I compare thee to a summer's day?
Thou art more lovely and more temperate:
Rough winds do shake the darling buds of May,
And summer's lease hath all too short a date:
Sometime too hot the eye of heaven shines,
And often is his gold complexion dimmed;
And ever fair from fair sometime declines,
By chance or nature's changing course untrimmed;
But thy eternal summer shall not fade,
Nor lose possession of that fair thou owest;
Nor shall Death brag thou wander'st in his shade,
When in eternal lines to time thou growest:
  So long as men can breathe, or eyes can see,
  So long lives this, and this gives life to thee.

Not Waving but Drowning

STEVIE SMITH

Nobody heard him, the dead man,
But still he lay moaning:
I was much further out than you thought
And not waving but drowning.

Poor chap, he always loved larking
And now he's dead
It must have been too cold for him his heart gave way,
They said.

Oh, no no no, it was too cold always
(Still the dead one lay moaning)
I was much too far out all my life
And not waving but drowning.

The Inchcape Rock

ROBERT SOUTHEY

No stir in the air, no stir in the sea,
The ship was still as she could be,
Her sails from heaven received no motion,
Her keel was steady in the ocean.

Without either sign or sound of their shock
The waves flowed over the Inchcape Rock;
So little they rose, so little they fell,
They did not move the Inchcape bell.

The Abbot of Aberbrothok
Had placed that bell on the Inchcape Rock;
On a buoy in the storm it floated and swung,
And over the waves its warning rung.

When the Rock was hid by the surge's swell,
The mariners heard the warning bell:
And then they knew the perilous rock,
And blessed the Abbot of Aberbrothok.

The sun in heaven was shining gay,
All things were joyful on that day;
The sea-birds screamed as they wheeled round,
And there was joyance in their sound.

The buoy of the Inchcape bell was seen
A darker speck on the ocean green;
Sir Ralph the Rover walked his deck,
And he fixed his eye on the darker speck.

He felt the cheering power of spring,
It made him whistle, it made him sing;
His heart was mirthful to excess,
But the Rover's mirth was wickedness.

His eye was on the Inchcape float;
Quoth he, 'My men, put out the boat,
And row me to the Inchcape Rock,
And I'll plague the Abbot of Aberbrothok.'

The boat is lowered, the boatmen row,
And to the Inchcape Rock they go;
Sir Ralph bent over from the boat,
And he cut the bell from the Inchcape float.

Down sunk the bell with a gurgling sound –
The bubbles rose and burst around;
Quoth Sir Ralph, 'The next who comes to the Rock
Won't bless the Abbot of Aberbrothok.'

Sir Ralph the Rover sailed away,
He scoured the seas for many a day;
And now grown rich with plundered store,
He steers his course for Scotland's shore.

So thick a haze o'erspreads the sky
They cannot see the sun on high;
The wind hath blown a gale all day,
At evening it hath died away.

On the deck the Rover takes his stand,
So dark it is they see no land.
Quoth Sir Ralph, 'It will be lighter soon,
For there is the dawn of the rising Moon.'

'Canst hear', said one, 'the breakers roar?
For methinks we should be near the shore.
Now where we are I cannot tell,
But I wish I could hear the Inchcape bell.'

They hear no sound – the swell is strong;
Though the wind hath fallen they drift along.
Till the vessel strikes with a shivering shock, –
'Oh! heavens! it is the Inchcape Rock!'

Sir Ralph the Rover tore his hair;
And curst himself in his despair;
The waves rush in on every side.
The ship is sinking beneath the tide.

But even in his dying fear
One dreadful sound could the Rover hear,
A sound as if, with the Inchcape bell,
The Devil below was ringing his knell.

The Vagabond

To *An Air of Schubert*

ROBERT LOUIS STEVENSON

Give to me the life I love,
  Let the lave go by me,
Give the jolly heaven above
  And the byway nigh me.
Bed in the bush with stars to see,
  Bread I dip in the river –
There's the life for a man like me,
  There's the life for ever.

Let the blow fall soon or late,
  Let what will be o'er me;
Give the face of earth around
  And the road before me.
Wealth I seek not, hope nor love,
  Nor a friend to know me;
All I seek, the heaven above
  And the road below me.

Or let autumn fall on me
  Where afield I linger,
Silencing the bird on tree,
  Biting the blue finger.
White as meal the frosty field –
  Warm the fireside haven –
Not to autumn will I yield,
  Not to winter even!

Let the blow fall soon or late,
  Let what will be o'er me;
Give the face of earth around,
  And the road before me.
Wealth I ask not, hope nor love,
  Nor a friend to know me;
All I ask, the heaven above
  And the road below me.

The Seed-Shop

MURIEL STUART

Here in a quiet and dusty room they lie,
  Faded as crumbled stone or shifting sand,
Forlorn as ashes, shrivelled, scentless, dry –
  Meadows and gardens running through my hand.

In this brown husk a dale of hawthorn dreams;
  A cedar in this narrow cell is thrust
That will drink deeply of a century's streams;
  These lilies shall make summer on my dust.

Here in their safe and simple house of death,
  Sealed in their shells, a million roses leap;
Here I can blow a garden with my breath,
  And in my hand a forest lies asleep.

from **The Brook**

ALFRED, LORD TENNYSON

I come from haunts of coot and hern,
  I make a sudden sally
And sparkle out among the fern,
  To bicker down a valley.

By thirty hills I hurry down,
  Or slip between the ridges,
By twenty thorps, a little town,
  And half a hundred bridges.

Till last by Philip's farm I flow
  To join the brimming river,
For men may come and men may go,
  But I go on for ever.

I chatter over stony ways,
  In little sharps and trebles,
I bubble into eddying bays,
  I babble on the pebbles.

With many a curve my banks I fret
  By many a field and fallow,
And many a fairy foreland set
  With willow-weed and mallow.

I chatter, chatter, as I flow
  To join the brimming river,
For men may come and men may go,
  But I go on for ever.

I wind about, and in and out,
  With here a blossom sailing,
And here and there a lusty trout,
  And here and there a grayling.

And here and there a foamy flake
  Upon me, as I travel
With many a silvery waterbreak
  Above the golden gravel.

And draw them all along, and flow
  To join the brimming river,
For men may come and men may go,
  But I go on for ever.

I steal by lawns and grassy plots,
  I slide by hazel covers;
I move the sweet forget-me-nots
  That grow for happy lovers.

I slip, I slide, I gloom, I glance,
  Among my skimming swallows;
I make the netted sunbeam dance
  Against my sandy shallows.

I murmur under moon and stars
  In brambly wildernesses;
I linger by my shingly bars;
  I loiter round my cresses;

And out again I curve and flow
  To join the brimming river,
For men may come and men may go,
  But I go on for ever.

Black Monday Lovesong

A. S. J. TESSIMOND

In love's dances, in love's dances
One retreats and one advances.
One grows warmer and one colder,
One more hesitant, one bolder.
One gives what the other needed
Once, or will need, now unheeded.
One is clenched, compact, ingrowing
While the other's melting, flowing.
One is smiling and concealing
While the other's asking, kneeling.
One is arguing or sleeping
While the other's weeping, weeping.

And the question finds no answer
And the tune misleads the dancer
And the lost look finds no other
And the lost hand finds no brother
And the word is left unspoken
Till the theme and thread are broken.

When shall these divisions alter?
Echo's answer seems to falter:
'Oh the unperplexed, unvexed time
Next time ... one day ... one day ... next time!'

Fern Hill

DYLAN THOMAS

Now as I was young and easy under the apple boughs
About the lilting house and happy as the grass was green,
    The night above the dingle starry,
      Time let me hail and climb
     Golden in the heydays of his eyes,
And honoured among wagons I was prince of the apple
  towns
And once below a time I lordly had the trees and leaves
      Trail with daisies and barley
     Down the rivers of the windfall light.

And as I was green and carefree, famous among the barns
About the happy yard and singing as the farm was home,
    In the sun that is young once only,
      Time let me play and be
     Golden in the mercy of his means,
And green and golden I was huntsman and herdsman, the
  calves
Sang to my horn, the foxes on the hills barked clear and
      And the sabbath rang slowly
     In the pebbles of the holy streams.

All the sun long it was running, it was lovely, the hay
Fields high as the house, the tunes from the chimneys, it
  was air
    And playing, lovely and watery
      And fire green as grass.
     And nightly under the simple stars

As I rode to sleep the owls were bearing the farm away,
All the moon long I heard, blessed among stables, the
  night-jars
      Flying with the ricks, and the horses
        Flashing into the dark.

And then to awake, and the farm, like a wanderer white
With the dew, come back, the cock on his shoulder: it was all
      Shining, it was Adam and maiden,
        The sky gathered again
      And the sun grew round that very day,
So it must have been after the birth of the simple light
In the first, spinning place, the spellbound horses walking
  warm
      Out of the whinnying green stable
        On to the fields of praise.

And honoured among foxes and pheasants by the gay house
Under the new made clouds and happy as the heart was
  long,
      In the sun born over and over,
        I ran my heedless ways,
      My wishes raced through the house high hay
And nothing I cared, at my sky blue trades, that time allows
In all his tuneful turning so few and such morning songs
      Before the children green and golden
        Follow him out of grace.

Nothing I cared, in the lamb white days, that time would
  take me
Up to the swallow thronged loft by the shadow of my
  hand,
      In the moon that is always rising,
        Nor that riding to sleep

I should hear him fly with the high fields
And wake to the farm forever fled from the childless land.
Oh as I was young and easy in the mercy of his means,
Time held me green and dying
Though I sang in my chains like the sea.

Adlestrop

EDWARD THOMAS

Yes. I remember Adlestrop –
The name, because one afternoon
Of heat the express-train drew up there
Unwontedly. It was late June.

The steam hissed. Some one cleared his throat.
No one left and no one came
On the bare platform. What I saw
Was Adlestrop – only the name

And willows, willow-herb, and grass,
And meadowsweet, and haycocks dry,
No whit less still and lonely fair
Than the high cloudlets in the sky.

And for that minute a blackbird sang
Close by, and round him, mistier,
Farther and farther, all the birds
Of Oxfordshire and Gloucestershire.

Cynddylan On A Tractor

R. S. THOMAS

Ah, you should see Cynddylan on a tractor.
Gone the old look that yoked him to the soil;
He's a new man now, part of the machine,
His nerves of metal and his blood oil.
The clutch curses, but the gears obey
His least bidding, and lo, he's away
Out of the farmyard, scattering hens.
Riding to work now as a great man should,
He is the knight at arms breaking the fields'
Mirror of silence, emptying the wood
Of foxes and squirrels and bright jays.
The sun comes over the tall trees
Kindling all the hedges, but not for him
Who runs his engine on a different fuel.
And all the birds are singing, bills wide in vain,
As Cynddylan passes proudly up the lane.

Daisy

FRANCIS THOMPSON

Where the thistle lifts a purple crown
  Six foot out of the turf,
And the harebell shakes on the windy hill —
  O the breath of the distant surf! —

The hills look over on the South,
  And southward dreams the sea;
And with the sea-breeze hand in hand
  Came innocence and she.

Where 'mid the gorse the raspberry
  Red for the gatherer springs,
Two children did we stray and talk
  Wise, idle, childish things.

She listened with big-lipped surprise,
  Breast-deep 'mid flower and spine:
Her skin was like a grape, whose veins
  Run snow instead of wine.

She knew not those sweet words she spake,
  Nor knew her own sweet way;
But there's never a bird, so sweet a song
  Thronged in whose throat that day.

Oh, there were flowers in Storrington
  On the turf and on the spray;
But the sweetest flower on Sussex hills
  Was the Daisy-flower that day!

Her beauty smoothed earth's furrowed face!
  She gave me tokens three: —
A look, a word of her winsome mouth,
  And a wild raspberry.

A berry red, a guileless look,
  A still word, — strings of sand!
And yet they made my wild, wild heart
  Fly down to her little hand.

For, standing artless as the air,
  And candid as the skies,
She took the berries with her hand,
  And the love with her sweet eyes.

The fairest things have fleetest end,
  Their scent survives their close:
But the rose's scent is bitterness
  To him that loved the rose.

She looked a little wistfully,
  Then went her sunshine way: —
The sea's eye had a mist on it,
  And the leaves fell from the day.

She went her unremembering way,
  She went and left in me
The pang of all the partings gone,
  And partings yet to be.

She left me marvelling why my soul
  Was sad that she was glad;
At all the sadness in the sweet,
  The sweetness in the sad.

Still, still I seemed to see her, still
  Look up with soft replies,
And take the berries with her hand,
  And the love with her lovely eyes.

Nothing begins, and nothing ends,
  That is not paid with moan;
For we are born in other's pain,
  And perish in our own.

The Curfew Must Not Ring Tonight

ROSA HARTWICK THORPE

Slowly England's sun was setting o'er the hilltops far
away,
Filling all the land with beauty at the close of one sad
day;
And the last rays kissed the forehead of a man and
maiden fair,
He with footsteps slow and weary, she with sunny
floating hair;
He with bowed head, sad and thoughtful, she with lips
all cold and white,
Struggling to keep back the murmur, 'Curfew must not
ring tonight!'

'Sexton,' Bessie's white lips faltered, pointing to the
prison old,
With its turrets tall and gloomy, with its walls, dark,
damp and cold –
'I've a lover in the prison, doomed this very night to
die
At the ringing of the curfew, and no early help is
nigh.
Cromwell will not come till sunset'; and her face grew
strangely white
As she breathed the husky whisper, 'Curfew must not
ring tonight!'

'Bessie,' calmly spoke the sexton – and his accents
pierced her heart

Like the piercing of an arrow, like a deadly poisoned
  dart –
'Long, long years I've rung the curfew from that
  gloomy, shadowed tower;
Every evening, just at sunset, it has told the twilight
  hour;
I have done my duty ever, tried to do it just and
  right –
Now I'm old I still must do it: Curfew, girl, must ring
  tonight!'

Wild her eyes and pale her features, stern and white
  her thoughtful brow,
And within her secret bosom Bessie made a solemn
  vow.
She had listened while the judges read, without a tear
  or sigh,
'At the ringing of the curfew, Basil Underwood must
  die.'
And her breath came fast and faster, and her eyes grew
  large and bright,
As in undertone she murmured, 'Curfew must not ring
  tonight!'

With quick step she bounded forward, sprang within
  the old church door,
Left the old man treading slowly paths he'd often trod
  before;
Not one moment paused the maiden, but with eye and
  cheek aglow
Mounted up the gloomy tower, where the bell swung
  to and fro
As she climbed the dusty ladder, on which fell no ray
  of light,

Up and up, her white lips saying, 'Curfew shall not
   ring tonight!'

She has reached the topmost ladder, o'er her hangs the
   great dark bell;
Awful is the gloom beneath her like the pathway down
   to hell;
Lo, the ponderous tongue is swinging. 'Tis the hour of
   curfew now,
And the sight has chilled her bosom, stopped her
   breath and paled her brow;
Shall she let it ring? No, never! Flash her eyes with
   sudden light,
And she springs and grasps it firmly: 'Curfew shall not
   ring tonight!'

Out she swung, far out; the city seemed a speck of
   light below;
She 'twixt heaven and earth suspended as the bell
   swung to and fro;
And the sexton at the bell rope, old and deaf, heard
   not the bell,
But he thought it still was ringing fair young Basil's
   funeral knell.
Still the maiden clung more firmly, and, with
   trembling lips and white
Said, to hush her heart's wild beating, 'Curfew shall
   not ring tonight.'

It was o'er; the bell ceased swaying, and the maiden
   stepped once more
Firmly on the dark old ladder, where for hundred years
   before

Human foot had not been planted; but the brave deed
  she had done
Should be told long ages after – often as the setting
  sun
Should illume the sky with beauty, aged sires, with
  heads of white,
Long should tell the little children, 'Curfew did not
  ring that night.'

O'er the distant hills came Cromwell: Bessie sees him,
  and her brow,
Full of hope and full of gladness, has no anxious traces
  now.
At his feet she tells her story, shows her hands all
  bruised and torn;
And her face so sweet and pleading, yet with sorrow
  pale and worn,
Touched his heart with sudden pity – lit his eye with
  misty light;
'Go, your lover lives!' said Cromwell; 'Curfew shall not
  ring tonight!'

Romance

W. J. TURNER

When I was but thirteen or so
  I went into a golden land,
Chimborazo, Cotopaxi
  Took me by the hand.

My father died, my brother too,
  They passed like fleeting dreams.
I stood where Popocatapetl
  In the sunlight gleams.

I dimly heard the master's voice
  And boys far-off at play,
Chimborazo, Cotopaxi
  Had stolen me away.

I walked in a great golden dream
  To and fro from school –
Shining Popocatapetl
  The dusty streets did rule.

I walked home with a gold dark boy
  And never a word I'd say,
Chimborazo, Cotopaxi
  Had taken my speech away:

I gazed entranced upon his face
  Fairer than any flower –
O shining Popocatapetl
  It was thy magic hour:

The houses, people, traffic seemed
  Thin fading dreams by day,
Chimborazo, Cotopaxi
  They had stolen my soul away!

A Ballad Of Semmerwater

WILLIAM WATSON

Deep asleep, deep asleep,
Deep asleep it lies,
The still lake of Semmerwater
Under the still skies.

And many a fathom, many a fathom,
Many a fathom below,
In a king's tower and a queen's bower
The fishes come and go.

Once there stood by Semmerwater
A mickle town and tall;
King's tower and queen's bower,
And wakeman on the wall.

Came a begger halt and sore:
'I faint for lack of bread.'
King's tower and queen's bower
Cast him forth unfed.

He knocked at the door of the herdman's cot
The herdman's cot in the dale.
They gave him of their oatcake,
They gave him of their ale.

He has cursed aloud that city proud,
He has cursed it in its pride;
He has cursed it into Semmerwater
Down the brant hillside.

He has cursed it into Semmerwater
There to bide.

King's tower and queen's bower,
And a mickle town and tall;
By glimmer of scale and gleam of fir,
Folk have seen them all.
King's tower and queen's bower,
And weed and reed in the gloom;
And a lost city in Semmerwater,
Deep asleep till Doom.

Barbara Frietchie

JOHN GREENLEAF WHITTIER

Up from the meadows rich with corn,
Clear in the cool September morn,

The clustered spires of Frederick stand
Green-walled by the hills of Maryland.

Round about them orchards sweep,
Apple and peach tree fruited deep,

Fair as the garden of the Lord
To the eyes of the famished rebel horde,

On that pleasant morn of the early fall
When Lee marched over the mountain-wall;

Over the mountains winding down,
Horse and foot, into Frederick town.

Forty flags with their silver stars,
Forty flags with their crimson bars,

Flapped in the morning wind: the sun
Of noon looked down, and saw not one.

Up rose old Barbara Frietchie then,
Bowed with her fourscore years and ten;

Bravest of all in Frederick town,
She took up the flag the men hauled down;

In her attic window the staff she set,
To show that one heart was loyal yet.

Up the street came the rebel tread,
Stonewall Jackson riding ahead.

Under his slouched hat left and right
He glanced; the old flag met his sight.

'Halt!' – the dust-brown ranks stood fast.
'Fire!' – out blazed the rifle-blast.

It shivered the window, pane and sash;
It rent the banner with seam and gash.

Quick, as it fell, from the broken staff
Dame Barbara snatched the silken scarf.

She leaned far out on the window-sill,
And shook it forth with a royal will.

'Shoot, if you must, this old gray head,
But spare your country's flag,' she said.

A shade of sadness, a blush of shame,
Over the face of the leader came;

The nobler nature within him stirred
To life at that woman's deed and word;

'Who touches a hair of yon gray head
Dies like a dog! March on!' he said.

All day long through Frederick street
Sounded the tread of marching feet:

All day long that free flag tost
Over the heads of the rebel host.

Ever its torn folds rose and fell
On the loyal winds that loved it well;

And through the hill-gaps sunset light
Shone over it with a warm good-night.

Barbara Frietchie's work is o'er,
And the Rebel rides on his raids no more.

Honor to her! and let a tear
Fall, for her sake, on Stonewall's bier.

Over Barbara Frietchie's grave,
Flag of Freedom and Union, wave!

Peace and order and beauty draw
Round thy symbol of light and law;

And ever the stars above look down
On thy stars below in Frederick town!

Solitude

ELLA WHEELER WILCOX

Laugh, and the world laughs with you,
  Weep, and you weep alone,
For sad old earth must borrow its mirth,
  But has trouble enough of its own.
Sing, and the hills will answer;
  Sigh, it is lost on the air,
The echoes bound to a joyful sound,
  But shrink from voicing care.

Rejoice, and men will seek you;
  Grieve, and they turn and go.
They want full measure of all your pleasure.
  But they do not need your woe.
Be glad, and your friends are many,
  Be sad, and you lose them all;
There are none to decline your nectared wine,
  But alone you must drink life's gall.

Feast, and your halls are crowded,
  Fast, and the world goes by.
Succeed and give – and it helps you live,
  But no man can help you die;
There is room in the halls of pleasure
  For a large and lordly train,
But one by one we must all file on
  Through the narrow aisles of pain.

The Burial Of Sir John Moore After Corunna

CHARLES WOLFE

Not a drum was heard, not a funeral note,
  As his corse to the rampart we hurried;
Not a soldier discharged his farewell shot
  O'er the grave where our hero we buried.

We buried him darkly at dead of night,
  The sods with our bayonets turning,
By the struggling moonbeam's misty light
  And the lantern dimly burning.

No useless coffin enclosed his breast,
  Not in sheet or in shroud we wound him;
But he lay like a warrior taking his rest
  With his martial cloak around him.

Few and short were the prayers we said,
And we spoke not a word of sorrow;
But we steadfastly gazed on the face that was dead,
  And we bitterly thought of the morrow.

We thought, as we hollowed his narrow bed
  And smoothed down his lonely pillow,
That the foe and the stranger would tread o'er his
    head,
  And we far away on the billow!

Lightly they'll talk of the spirit that's gone,
  And o'er his cold ashes upbraid him –

But little he'll reck, if they let him sleep on
  In the grave where a Briton has laid him.

But half of our heavy task was done
  When the clock struck the hour for retiring;
And we heard the distant and random gun
  That the foe was sullenly firing.

Slowly and sadly we laid him down,
  From the field of his fame fresh and gory;
We carved not a line, and we raised not a stone,
  But we left him alone with his glory!

Lucy Gray; Or, Solitude

WILLIAM WORDSWORTH

Oft I had heard of Lucy Gray:
And, when I crossed the wild,
I chanced to see at break of day
The solitary child.

No mate, no comrade Lucy knew;
She dwelt on a wide moor,
– The sweetest thing that ever grew
Beside a human door!

You yet may spy the fawn at play,
The hare upon the green;
But the sweet face of Lucy Gray
Will never more be seen.

'To-night will be a stormy night –
You to the town must go;
And take a lantern, Child, to light
Your mother through the snow.'

'That, Father! will I gladly do:
'Tis scarcely afternoon –
The minister-clock has just struck two,
And yonder is the moon!'

At this the Father raised his hook,
And snapped a faggot-band;
He plied his work; – and Lucy took
The lantern in her hand.

Not blither is the mountain roe:
With many a wanton stroke
Her feet disperse the powdery snow,
That rises up like smoke.

The storm came on before its time:
She wandered up and down;
And many a hill did Lucy climb:
But never reached the town.

The wretched parents all that night
Went shouting far and wide;
But there was neither sound nor sight
To serve them for a guide.

At day-break on a hill they stood
They overlooked the moor;
And thence they saw the bridge of wood,
A furlong from their door.

They wept – and, turning homeward, cried,
'In heaven we all shall meet;'
– When in the snow the mother spied
The print of Lucy's feet.

Then downwards from the steep hill's edge
They traced the footmarks small;
And through the broken hawthorne hedge,
And by the long stone-wall;

And then an open field they crossed:
The marks were still the same;
They tracked them on, nor ever lost;
And to the bridge they came.

They followed from the snowy bank
Those footmarks, one by one,
Into the middle of the plank;
And further there were none!

— Yet some maintain that to this day
She is a living child;
That you may see sweet Lucy Gray
Upon the lonesome wild.

O'er rough and smooth she trips along,
And never looks behind;
And sings a solitary song
That whistles in the wind.

The Lake Isle Of Innisfree

W. B. YEATS

I will arise and go now, and go to Innisfree,
And a small cabin build there, of clay and wattles
   made:
Nine bean-rows will I have there, a hive for the
   honey-bee,
And live alone in the bee-loud glade.
And I shall have some peace there, for peace comes
   dropping slow,
Dropping from the veils of the morning to where the
   cricket sings;
There midnight's all a-glimmer, and noon a purple
   glow,
And evening full of the linnet's wings.

I will arise and go now, for always night and day
I hear lake water lapping with low sounds by the
   shore;
While I stand on the roadway, or on the pavements
   grey,
I hear it in the deep heart's core.

Acknowledgments

The editor and publishers wish to thank the following for permission to use copyright material:

Martin Armstrong, for an extract from 'Miss Thompson Goes Shopping'. Copyright © Martin Armstrong 1920, by permission of PFD on behalf of the Estate of the author; W. H. Auden, for 'If I Could Tell You' from *Collected Poems* by W. H. Auden. Copyright © 1976 by Edward Mendelson, William Meredith and Monro K. Spears, Executors of the Estate of the author, by permission of Faber and Faber Ltd and Random House, Inc; Hilaire Belloc, for 'Tarantella' from *Complete Verse* by Hilaire Belloc, by permission of PFD on behalf of the Estate of the author; John Betjeman, for 'Diary of a Church Mouse' from *Collected Poems* by John Betjeman, by permission of John Murray (Publishers) Ltd; Charles Causley, for 'Timothy Winters' from *Collected Poems* by Charles Causley, Macmillan, by permission of David Higham Associates on behalf of the author; Max Ehrmann, for 'Desiderata' from *The Desiderata of Happiness* by Max Ehrmann. Copyright © 1927 by Max Ehrmann, by permission of Robert L. Bell, Melrose, USA; Eleanor Farjeon, for 'Mrs Malone' from *Silver Sand and Snow* by Eleanor Farjeon, by permission of David Higham Associates on behalf of the author; W. W. Gibson, for 'The Ice Cart' from *Collected Poems* by W. W. Gibson, by permission of Macmillan, London; A. E. Housman, for 'Loveliest of Trees, The Cherry Now' from *A Shropshire Lad* by A. E. Housman, by permission of The Society of Authors as the Literary Representative of the Estate of the author; Jenny Joseph, for 'Warning', by permission of John Johnson (Authors' Agent) Ltd on behalf of the author; Rudyard Kipling, for 'The Glory of the Garden', by permission of A. P.

161